SMALLBORE RIFLE
SHOOTING
A PRACTICAL GUIDE

SMALLBORE RIFLE SHOOTING

A PRACTICAL GUIDE

Christopher Fenning
Foreword by Nick Clark

THE CROWOOD PRESS

First published in 2010 by
The Crowood Press Ltd
Ramsbury, Marlborough
Wiltshire SN8 2HR

www.crowood.com

This impression 2014

British Library Cataloguing-in-Publication Data
A catalogue record for this book is available from the British Library.

ISBN 978 1 84797 226 2

Disclaimer
The author and the publisher do not accept any responsibility in any manner whatsoever for any error or omission, or any loss, damage, injury, adverse outcome, or liability of any kind incurred as a result of the use of any of the information contained in this book, or reliance upon it. If in doubt about any aspect of small-bore rifle shooting, readers are advised to seek professional advice.

Acknowledgements
This book is a gathering together of the thoughts and experience from all my years of shooting and this in turn is the experience of all those who have taught me how to shoot. Although the words written on these pages were written by me the content came from all the coaches, tutors and people who I have had the pleasure and privilege of shooting with, and I would like to express my thanks to everyone who I have learnt from for helping me, possibly unknowingly, to write this book.

As a personal note I would like to thank Nick Clark for his fantastic support and guidance. Nick has reviewed the content many times, suggesting improvements and changes as well as taking almost all of the photographs. This thanks should also be extended to his wife Chris for the fabulous chicken curry that sustained through the long nights of proof reading.

A huge thank you also goes to Phil Frost, Jon Weir and Peter Weir who spent many hours on a studio floor posing for the images used in this book as well as being the test subjects for many of the practice exercises. Without their patience and eagerness to help this book would not have been completed. Many of the photos were taken at Farm Studios near Bristol; we had a great day there and Nick Pitt was very helpful in setting up lighting and providing guidance on the day. 'On location' shots have come from my home club of Bristol Invicta and also from Chippenham Rifle and Pistol club: thanks to these clubs for allowing the photos to be used.

Julie Simmons, Keith Simmons and Max Frost suggested content and loaned items of kit for the pictures. Their suggestions resulted in entire chapters being added and without their help this book would not be comprehensive. Writing a book for the first time would have been far more daunting had it not been for the staff at The Crowood Press guiding me through the process of preparing a book for print.

Finally, I would like to say thank you to Danielle Briggs who not only encouraged me to write this book but also provided me with the opportunity and the time in which I could write, sometimes from great distance.

Typeset by Jean Cussons Typesetting, Diss, Norfolk

Printed and bound in India by Replika Press Pvt. Ltd.

CONTENTS

FOREWORD

Throughout history marksmanship has been a highly prized and sought-after skill developed during many hours of dedicated training and practice. In medieval times archers developed and perfected the techniques necessary to draw a longbow and release an arrow with deadly accuracy and a force that could penetrate the armour plating of opposing armies, as was demonstrated during the battle of Agincourt in 1415 when many a French knight perished.

Such was the importance of marksmanship that a law was passed in 1252 requiring every man between the ages of fifteen and sixty to equip himself with a bow. Training sessions were ordered by law, usually held on a Sunday. In many villages today there is still a street called The Butts, which marks the place where archers practised their skill, shooting at targets – the butts.

Over time the need for archers has diminished and with advances in technology many new weapons have been developed, including the small-bore rifle. While British law does not prescribe weekly target practice, there remains within many a desire to master the skills of marksmanship. Today these skills are demonstrated at the Olympic and Commonwealth Games (along with other worldwide events), where Great Britain is represented by some of the most accomplished shooters in the land.

In past times, when many could not read or write, the skills of marksmanship were passed by word of mouth and improvement was relatively slow, with learning often limited to the knowledge of those within the village. As time has progressed so has the method of retaining and passing on knowledge.

The author has brought together many different pieces of information based upon his own experience and that of others, and has sorted them into a clear and logical order to provide an introduction into small-bore target rifle shooting, setting out the preliminary steps required for those that wish to start upon a journey of learning.

It is clear that the book will help a novice shooter learn the basic skills required to hit a target consistently and with accuracy. It is also recognized that the author has taken time to ensure that the experience is enjoyable, with a number of exercises to test the understanding and competence of a particular skill, which will benefit both the novice and experienced shooter.

Nicholas Clark
Great Britain and England
representative (1993–2008)

INTRODUCTION

It is perhaps a little known fact that shooting is a surprisingly common activity. There are over 600 clubs with more than 10,000 people shooting small-bore rifle on a regular basis in the United Kingdom alone. For some, shooting is a recreational sport to be enjoyed with friends and provides an environment to meet like-minded people. For others, it is an intense challenge requiring discipline and effort with the goal of competing at club, county or international level.

Rifle shooting is one of a small number of sports open to almost anyone, irrespective of any disabilities, age, gender and fitness, factors that do not by themselves define who will be good or bad at shooting as they do with some other sports (although there are limitations to the type of shooting that can be done by people with a criminal record).

Each person takes something different from the sport. Some find it helps with concentration and patience; for others it provides an experience that is very different from their usual day to day activities.

ABOUT THIS BOOK

Regardless of how old someone might be when they start learning to shoot, there is always a first time that they pick up a rifle and learn the basics of how to fire a shot. This book aims to take the reader from that shot onward, through increasing levels of understanding and competence, until they are able to shoot in competitions. It will offer advice and answers to common (and some not so common) questions, while also providing a comprehensive resource for club instructors and intermediate shooters who want to remind themselves of the basic techniques.

A small-bore rifle shooter wearing full prone position kit.

The book covers the key aspects of small-bore rifle shooting in the prone position (lying down); positional shooting (standing and kneeling) is not covered here. Newcomers to the sport may be surprised at the level of detail given in each chapter (there is, for example, a chapter almost entirely about to how to breathe). Such detail may seem daunting but is presented in a way that should be easy to digest. Don't worry if the terminology is new, as it will all be covered in the first few chapters. The first chapter is a brief history of small-bore rifle shooting, covering the key milestones and influences that led to the sport we have today. The next few chapters cover how to find a club and arrange a first shooting session, and then what to do and expect on first using a rifle. Understanding what is likely to happen and what the first session will involve should mean there are no surprises and that the session is both beneficial and fun.

For most newcomers to the sport, learning to shoot with a supported rifle (resting on a box, a sandbag or such) provides an introduction to the core skills of shooting. Chapter Four takes the reader through the early stages of learning to shoot, introducing key skills and providing some practice exercises to help demonstrate the theory.

The next step for the novice is shooting without a support. Chapters Five and Six guide the reader through the transition from shooting with a stand to comfortably shooting with a jacket. In this case the word 'comfortable' means physical comfort from lying on the ground while holding the rifle, as well as the mental comfort, or confidence, to be had from knowing that the right thing is being done when taking each shot.

Learning to shoot, as with every other sport, relies as much on practical experience as on the theory. Throughout the book the theory is supported with exercises and activities. Chapter Seven provides a series of exercises that help demonstrate the information being described and gives step by step guidance on how to improve skills.

The next chapter introduces sight adjustment and helps the reader progress towards shooting at scored targets. Chapter Nine describes the set-up and use of a spotting scope, while the following chapter covers the types of scored targets and how to work out the scores. Care and maintenance of the equipment is an important part of this precision sport and Chapter Eleven gives practical advice on rifle cleaning.

All this leads toward the excitement of confidently shooting in competitions. Information about how competitions are run, entry requirements and general advice on making things just a little easier are all covered in Chapter Twelve.

In theory this book should end there with the reader happily shooting in competitions. Some extra chapters have been added, however, offering guidance on what the reader might encounter next, such as buying kit and how to move into outdoor shooting and how the weather can have an effect on this.

Remember, this book is a guide to help readers with little or no prior knowledge of the sport, but it can never be a substitute for physically going to a club and actually shooting.

Measurements

Both imperial and metric measurements appear in this book. Shooting distances for standard competition are between 15 and 25 yards indoors, and fixed at 50m and 100 yards outdoors. There is also a 50 yard outdoor event, but this is unusual and not usually a standard event, so it is not covered here.

Calibres are in inches (.22) but distances relating to missing the target are in millimetres.

This can all appear a little inconsistent, but that is the nature of this sport!

CHAPTER 1

SMALL-BORE RIFLE SHOOTING: A BRIEF HISTORY

Small-bore rifle shooting involves the use of .22 calibre target rifles firing .22 rimfire ammunition at paper or cardboard targets at distances from 15 yards up to 100 yards. The practical skills involved are very similar to those used for both full-bore and air rifle shooting with the main difference being the type of rifle and ammunition used.

Rifle shooting originated as a skill used by hunters and the military as a modernization of the marksmanship skills previously used by archers. It developed into a competitive civilian sport at international level during the late nineteenth and the early twentieth centuries. This chapter describes the path taken from its early beginnings through to the sport recognized today, covering the principal events and governing bodies as well as some of the main manufacturers of small-bore rifles and equipment.

BEFORE 1900

During the nineteenth century shooting clubs and organizations developed into national shooting federations. Switzerland formed one of the earliest federations in the 1820s, England, France and Germany formed national Associations in the middle of the century, shortly followed by the United States in 1871. It was not until the start of the next century that an international federation would be created.

International shooting competitions were first held at the 1896 Summer Olympics, and the first World Championships were held a year later in 1897. The inclusion of shooting at these events is largely believed to be the responsibility of French pistol champion Pierre de Coubertin, who was one of the founders of the modern Olympic Games.

The rifles used in competitions were either military or hunting rifles and the companies who currently make small-bore rifles for sports shooting were only just starting out. The Anschütz family business was founded in 1856 and at first produced mainly pistols and shotguns; the company did not start designing and making target rifles until almost 100 years later. Carl Walther began his trade in 1886, working closely with his family on the design and manufacture of target rifles.

1900–10

In the United Kingdom rifle shooting as a civilian sport grew from a military requirement. Around the time of the Second Boer War (1899–1902) it was believed necessary to increase the shooting ability of the general population in the event that the regular army could not withstand an invasion. There were comparatively few formally recognized rifle clubs and those that did exist were associated with the Volunteers (the organization now known as the Territorial Army), using military rifles on outdoor ranges. These were often located a long way from towns or cities and travelling to them was quite expensive. With ammunition costs on top of the travel, not many members of the general public could afford to shoot.

In 1900 the British Rifle League was created, followed in 1901 by the Society of Working Men's Rifle Clubs (SMRC). It was decided that civilians could learn to shoot using the comparatively cheap 'miniature' (small-bore) rifles and ammunition instead of the standard service rifle. This made shooting more accessible to the wider population by reducing the travel required to get to ranges. Rifles of .22 calibre were readily available at modest cost: a sporting type rifle could then be purchased for £1 or less at the time (roughly equal to £100 today). It was also easier to comply with safety requirements for rifle ranges intended for the smaller rifles than those meant for high-calibre service rifles.

The cost of a gun licence at the time was 10 shillings per year, almost £50 today, and this presented a considerable barrier to shooting for most people. When the rules changed in 1906, members of a club affiliated to the British Rifle League were exempt from paying the licence fee, thus making shooting as a hobby even more accessible.

The first international governing body for shooting appeared in 1907 when eight national associations joined together to create the Union International de Tir (UIT, known in English as the ISU). New members joined over the following years. In 1998 the organization's name was changed to the International Shooting Sport Federation (ISSF).

The end of the decade also saw the creation of County Associations in the UK and the start of the annual Queen's Cup competition.

1910–30

By the outbreak of war in 1914 a large number of UK civilians had learnt the skills of shooting through clubs supported by the SMRC and many were willing to put these skills to use in the service of their country. The 1916 Olympic Games, intended to be held in Berlin, did not take place. Although some international matches were held in 1916, the ISU member countries voted to dissolve the committee.

Following the end of the war in 1918 rifle clubs in the UK suffered from a combination of increased legislation for shooting and a reduced number of club members, many of whom had been killed in action. The SMRC continued to work to increase the interest in small-bore rifle shooting and slowly over time the clubs began to revive.

The ISU was re-formed in 1920 with additional members from some of the countries newly created in Europe. The twenty-one different shooting events included in the 1920 Olympics was the highest number since the Games began; this was followed in 1921 with a decision by the International Olympic Committee (IOC) to allow the ISU to govern the shooting events in the future games, thus starting the relationship that continues to exist in 2010.

The end of this period saw increasing interest in small-bore shooting and attendance at national and international events was very good. However, this caused some problems for the new relationship between the ISU and IOC, since ISU World Championship events awarded prize money and this went against the IOC amateur standards. The disagreement between the two governing bodies was such that shooting was excluded from the 1928 Olympic Games in Amsterdam.

During this time both Anschütz and Walther continued to design and manufacture new types of gun, but as yet neither had started to work on small-bore target rifles. Walther developed shotguns and pistols including the famous PP range, such as the PPK used in the earlier James Bond books, and Anschütz continued to make pistols and military rifles.

1930–50

Following an appeal by the ISU, shooting was reinstated as an event in the 1932 Los Angeles Olympic Games. However, the number of events was reduced to two, with only a single rifle event. The attendance at the games was low and many of the best marksmen in the world were missing because they had won money prizes in competitions and thus did not meet the IOC amateur standards required for the Olympics.

In the years leading up to the Second World War the World Championships provided the stage for the first woman entrant in an international event: Catherine Woodring shot for the USA team and helped the team win the gold medal. During the same period shooting in the UK once again grew into a common sport, with more than 2,000 clubs and sixty County Associations across the country.

With Europe once more at war the number of affiliated clubs in the United Kingdom increased, aided by the formation of the Home Guard, which was responsible for the foundation of many of the clubs that exist today. The Secretary of State for War paid tribute in the House of Commons to the SMRC's role in assisting with training and range certification work. By the end of 1945 there were more than 4,000 affiliated clubs and other organizations in the SMRC, of which 1,000 were former Home Guard units. In 1947 the SMRC changed its name to the National Small-bore Rifle Association (NSRA), which remains the governing body for small-bore rifle shooting in the UK.

The post-war years saw the reappearance of international rifle events, although the number of shooting events at the 1948 Olympic Games in London was still far below the pre-1924 high of more than twenty. It was also a fresh start for two of today's main rifle manufacturers, Anschütz and Walther. Both companies suffered at the end of the war and had to restart almost from scratch, adopting new company names that differed slightly from the original name. Anschütz returned to designing and repairing pistols with a small operation that employed fewer than ten people. This new start was particularly difficult for Walther, which went from a pre-war high of more than 2,500 employees to being just Fritz Walther with a small case of design drawings and patents. Before the war the Walther business had manufactured both weapons and early calculators, and it was the calculator business that provided the basis for the new company.

The year 1950 proved to be pivotal for both companies: Anschütz rifle sales gained momentum after successes with their new rifles at target shooting events, while Walther expanded the business to once again design and build air rifles by the end of the year.

SINCE 1950

With the sport fully established on the world stage, the next half century provided the developments that turned the sport into what it is today. New competitions appeared at both National and International levels, more event types were added to existing competitions and new associations formed to help facilitate the development of new and experienced shooters.

In the UK, the post-war years saw a decline in the number of clubs affiliated to the NSRA. As the Home Guard units disbanded and the core purpose of small-bore rifle shooting changed from the need to defend the country into a solely recreational sport, the total number of clubs dropped to around 1,000. Despite this reduction, shooting remains a very popular sport with thousands of people competing at levels from beginner through to world class.

Gender equality was established in shooting and in the mid-1960s the ISU recognized all of its open events as 'mixed' events where women could participate with men. The IOC also agreed to apply this standard to Olympic shooting events. For four Olympiads, from 1968 through 1980, the Olympic shooting events were mixed, with opportunities for women and men to participate regardless of gender. This has now developed into separate events for men and women, as seen in today's events.

Rifle design developed steadily as manufacturers worked with world-class shooters to refine the designs. Some notable success were achieved in the 1960s and 1970s using the Anschütz Match rifle. Toward the end of the century advances in materials and manufacturing techniques enabled designers to increase the levels of precision in their rifles to such an extent that, when coupled with the ever increasing skill of the shooters, it became harder to distinguish between the top shots at events. The solution to this difficulty was a reduction in diameter of the target by roughly 20 per cent. This change made it harder to hit the centre ring of the target and easier to differentiate between the scores of the top shooters. Today there are a number of core rifle designers and manufacturers providing complete rifles with MEC, Feinwerkbau, HPS and others joining the already established Walther and Anschütz.

The NSRA is the governing body for small-bore shooting in the UK, and is one of a number of organizations established to promote, support and encourage the range of shooting disciplines available in the United Kingdom today.

CHAPTER 2

GETTING STARTED

Small-bore rifle shooting is a sport open to almost anybody. The main exception is that anyone with a criminal conviction is not permitted to shoot small-bore rifles, although other options, such as air rifle and air pistol, can be pursued instead. It is mandatory that all newcomers to the sport join a club as a probationary member and undergo a police check.

Having decided to try shooting as a sport, the next step is to find a club that can provide the introduction and instruction a beginner requires. This process is fairly straightforward and this chapter provides information that can help the reader to locate, contact and arrange a first session at a local club.

FINDING AND SELECTING A CLUB

Finding a Local Rifle Club

Small-bore rifle shooting is a very common sport that is competed at both the Commonwealth and Olympic Games, but it is not widely advertised. Despite this lack of public knowledge, the United Kingdom has a large number of small-bore rifle clubs with more than 600 clubs shooting on a regular basis, with an average of twenty members per club.

Newcomers to the sport should look for Home Office-approved clubs. Although there are some clubs in the UK without Home Office approval,

the regulations governing them may not provide the best experience or easiest access to the sport.

Often the locations of rifle clubs are not broadly publicized for security reasons, but clubs are relatively common and exist in both obvious and unexpected places. Some clubs are tucked away in old quarries or on farms out in the countryside, some share facilities with local Army or Territorial Army units, and some are in the middle of residential areas surrounded by houses.

There are a number of resources available to help locate clubs in a specific area of the country. Local authorities and the internet are the two best options, with lists of clubs and their contact details available to the public. A basic internet search of 'town + rifle club' might return some information, but not all clubs have websites and those that do may not show up in the first few pages of search results. Lists of clubs are produced and maintained by different organizations and some of the best resources are:

www.nsra.co.uk. The website of the National Small-bore Rifle Association (NSRA). This has a good database of clubs by region and county. All of the clubs listed here are affiliated to the NSRA.

www.small-borerifle.co.uk. This is an independent website that carries a comprehensive list of clubs, including those that are not affiliated to the NSRA.

Local authorities. All local authorities maintain lists of sports clubs in their area and information can be found on their websites or by contacting them directly.

Clubs are spread all over the UK and searches might show that only one club is located within a reasonable travelling distance, but it is equally possible for there to be several clubs to choose from.

Types of Club

Home Office approved. These clubs are registered with, and have been approved by, the Home Office and operate in a manner that enables newcomers to the sport to shoot as probationary members while learning.

Non-Home Office approved. Clubs with fewer than ten members are permitted to operate within specific guidelines, for example, all members must have their own Firearm Certificate and no weapons or ammunition can be stored at the range. More information on such clubs is available from the Home Office.

NSRA affiliated. A club can be affiliated to the NSRA irrespective of whether it is Home Office approved. The NSRA affiliation gives clubs access to a wide range of competitions and qualifications and provides insurance for the club members and third parties.

Selecting a Club

Having identified clubs within a specific area the next important step is to contact the club (or clubs) and arrange a visit to their range. The directories and information sources used to locate clubs (as described above) will generally include details of the club secretary or another person to contact about enquiries. If contact details are unavailable it is often possible to ask for information at another club in the same area.

Clubs within close geographical distance often compete against each other and will know the right person to phone or email. If all else fails the NSRA can be very helpful in initiating contact with a club.

The reader is encouraged to make enquires at a number of clubs in order to help choose the most appropriate. Some questions that could be asked are:

- Is the club Home Office approved and what is the expiry date for the approval?
- Number of members?
- Is the club a member of the NSRA?
- How many qualified range conducting officers, club instructors and club coaches does the club have?
- If the applicant is under eighteen years old and will not be shooting with a parent or guardian present, have the club coaches been CRB checked?

Clubs vary in size and will have different numbers of qualified instructors and range officers. These differences can have an effect on the type of experience a new shooter will have. It is recommended that newcomers to the sport aim to join Home Office-approved clubs with NSRA membership, because this provides the greatest opportunity to develop in the sport and allows access to a wide range of events and courses. Clubs with few members can be just as good as those with large memberships, however, since the availability of instructors for new starters will be an important factor. It is possible to change clubs and this provides the opportunity to learn at a club with an instructor and then move to another club that may be more convenient for travel or other reasons.

Sometimes clubs may not be able to take new starters, perhaps owing to a shortage of equipment, instructors or space necessary to provide the support required by a newcomer to the sport. It is rare that a club will turn away someone who is interested in shooting without a very good reason; usually there will be a waiting list that can be joined, or the club may suggest other clubs in the area that do have space.

ARRANGING A FIRST SESSION AND PROBATIONARY MEMBERSHIP

People who want to try shooting and who do not already hold a Firearm Certificate must apply for probationary membership to a club before they are able to shoot. The probation application form, which should be obtained from the club prior to the first session, requires details about the applicant including their full name, address, signature of parent or guardian (if the applicant is under the age of sixteen) and details of two independent referees. These will be forwarded to the police and references will be sought. This initial information check and the police process should not take long as each club should have a designated police liaison officer whom they can contact regularly.

The probationary period lasts a minimum of three months, after which the probationer can apply to become a full member of the club. There is no set fee for probationary membership although there may be a charge and the clubs will make this clear to the applicant. Some clubs may provide a free first session but most will charge a small fee to cover the cost of the ammunition. Sessions may be held on specific nights of the week, once a month or at any time convenient for the set-up of the club in question.

The first session should include a safety briefing, an introduction to the rifle and other shooting equipment, as well as some of the basics of shooting. The reader should be aware that not all clubs will allow newcomers to shoot on their first session and instead topics on safety, orientation, and theory will be covered; shooting can begin at the second session. This process can

be beneficial if probationary membership has been applied for but not confirmed, since it allows some additional time for the membership to be processed and still provides benefit to the new shooter through the theory lessons.

Always remember to take a notebook and a pen – it is very important that shooters keep good records of what they do right from the start. The notebook will be used to keep records of the kit used, the set-up and measurements of the different components of the rifles, and also to track the topics covered in each shooting session.

OPTIONS OPEN TO YOUNGER SHOOTERS

There are other options available to those under eighteen years of age who wish to learn to shoot but are unable to join a small-bore club. Organizations such as the Scouts, Guides, Adventure Scouts and the Cadet Forces (such as the ATC and CCF) can often provide a fun and safe environment in which to learn to shoot, as well as providing a multitude of other activities.

Many of these groups offer air rifle shooting and some also offer small-bore rifle shooting at their own facilities or through use of a local small-bore rifle club. Air rifle shooting shares many of the skills required for small-bore rifle shooting. Key differences are in the storage, ownership and location of use of air rifles and their ammunition. Air rifle shooting can be just as enjoyable and equally satisfying to master, and the skills can be transferred to small-bore shooting at a later date.

Shooting can also form part of a Duke of Edinburgh's Award scheme, through which it is possible to undertake a short course of about ten weeks that can provide an introduction into a lifelong interest in the sport. When contacting a club about learning to shoot for any scheme like this make sure this intention is clearly stated at the start.

CHAPTER 3

THE FIRST TIME WITH A RIFLE

The first time anyone lies down to shoot with a rifle should be both a fun and safe experience. There is plenty of theory that can be given to someone before they start shooting – about ammunition grades, rifle types, techniques for breathing and trigger release among others – but at this early stage most people are eager to find out if shooting is a sport that they will enjoy. The best way to do that is to get down behind a rifle and shoot at a target or two.

This chapter provides an introduction to the

rifle, the type of kit that is likely to be used during the first sessions, safety and a short guide on how to take the first shots with a rifle. It will also suggest what to expect from the whole experience, bearing in mind that it is about having fun as well as being safe and accurate.

In addition to the mandatory safety briefing and orientation of the rifle some basic theory should be provided to a new shooter before any shots are fired. The theory covers the basics of

Shooting for the first time will usually involve a rifle supported on a stand. The stand shown here is a bench-rest stand, although other types can be used instead.

Examples of rifles that may be available at clubs. Newer rifles are at the back and the more common, older models of rifle at the front.

loading and aiming, the use of the trigger and what to expect when the shot is fired. Theory is important in order for the shooter to get the most out of their first shots, but a balance should be found between providing useful information and allowing the shooter to get hands-on practical experience.

EQUIPMENT

Getting to Know the Kit

It may seem odd to take a slight step away from shooting for a moment in order to make an analogy about learning to drive, but it will help set the scene for the type, age and quality of kit that will usually be available for use at clubs.

No matter what their age, gender or any other differentiating factor, the first time someone learns to drive they are unlikely to be put behind the wheel of a top-end sports car such as a Ferrari. Certainly the cars used by driving schools are reasonable vehicles with all the required safety standards, but brand new super cars are something they are not. This is the same with shooting: the first time a new shooter turns up at a club they are unlikely to be presented with a state-of-the-art match rifle. What is more likely is that an older model rifle

will be made available for the new shooter to 'try their hand'. These rifles might not look out of place in a photo taken in the 1950s, but these appearances can be deceiving because the rifles will still shoot with great accuracy if handled properly – and don't be surprised if someone launches into a story about how 'old Bob' once used that very rifle to shoot to glory in the summer season sometime back in the past. There are many stories of this kind at clubs and one day the present reader might well find themselves telling the stories instead of listening to them.

A key thing to remember is that at this early stage of learning to shoot, the quality of kit will have the least bearing on the quality of the shooting. It is the actions of the person holding the rifle that will have the greatest effect on the accuracy of each shot: the old analogy of the workman and his tools fits well here.

The Rifle

Much of the information here will use terminology referring to the different parts of a rifle. It will be beneficial to the reader if some time is spent getting to know the names and purpose of these different parts before continuing with the rest of the book.

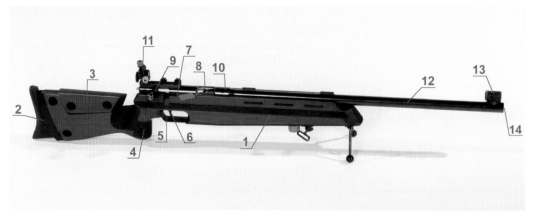

Bolt action rifle components: (1) Stock; (2) Butt; (3) Cheek piece; (4) Pistol grip; (5) Trigger guard; (6) Trigger; (7) Action; (8) Breech; (9) Bolt; (10) Chamber; (11) Rear sight; (12) Barrel; (13) Foresight; (14) Muzzle.

Stock. The body of the rifle. Historically this is made from a single, solid piece of wood (walnut or ash), but modern rifles can have laminated wood or aluminium stocks and can be made up of multiple sections. This is the part of the rifle that the shooter will have contact with while holding the rifle.

Butt. This part of the stock sits against the shooter's shoulder when the rifle is held.

Cheek piece. The cheek of the shooter will be placed on/against this while firing and it provides a platform to help align the eye with the sights.

Pistol grip. The firing hand of the shooter lightly grips the pistol grip and provides the correct position for the trigger finger.

Trigger guard. A protective guard that is fitted to the stock and prevents the trigger from being knocked or damaged accidentally when the rifle is being moved.

Trigger. The device that translates the motion of the finger into the firing of the rifle and is fixed to the underside of the action.

Action. A metal housing fixed into the stock that connects the trigger, bolt and barrel together.

Breech. An opening in the top of the action where the ammunition is loaded into the rifle. This is the entry point to the chamber.

Bolt. A device used to push the round fully into the chamber, providing a seal around the end of the chamber during firing. It also holds the firing pin. After the round has been fired the bolt is used to extract the empty ammunition case from the chamber and eject it from the rifle.

Chamber. The ammunition will be sealed into the chamber prior to firing. The chamber also contains the force of the explosion used to propel the bullet through the barrel.

Rear sight. Used in conjunction with the foresight to aim the rifle at the target. It is positioned on top of the action about 7.5cm (3in) in front of the eye that is used for aiming.

Barrel. The metal tube that connects into the action and sits on top of the stock. The inside of the tube has a spiral twist cut into it, which makes the bullet spin as it flies through the air.

Foresight. The foresight is fitted to the muzzle end of the barrel and is lined up with the rear sight and the target to aim the rifle accurately.

Muzzle. The end of the barrel where the bullet will emerge when the rifle is fired.

Bolt Action and Martini Action Rifles

There are many types of small-bore rifle available, but new shooters will usually come across two main types: 'bolt action' and 'Martini action' rifles. They share similar characteristics, for example, they both have a barrel, a stock, sights and a trigger, but the key difference is in the way the ammunition is loaded before firing and how the empty shell is then ejected after firing.

The main difference between a bolt action and Martini action rifle is that the latter does not have a bolt. Instead of using a bolt to seal the round in the chamber, there is a lever that closes the breech and 'cocks' the firing pin. When the round has been fired the lever is used again to open the breech and remove and eject the empty ammunition case from the chamber.

Aside from the method used to load and eject the round from the rifle there are no other obvious differences between bolt action and Martini action rifles and both can be used to shoot very accurately.

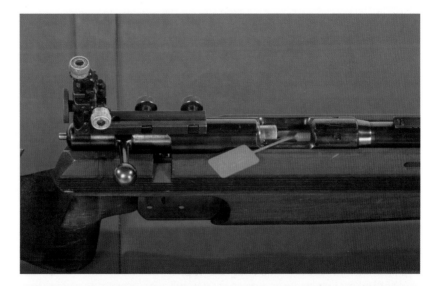

Bolt action rifle.

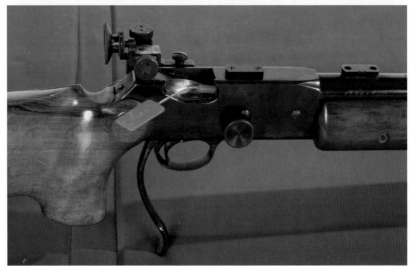

A Martini action rifle uses a lever to close the breech before firing and to open it again to eject the round.

Newer model rifles provide greater flexibility for the shooter. Adjustable sections can be changed to fit the shooter's own particular body shape.

New Rifles

The basic elements of modern rifles are the same as for older models. All rifles include a barrel, stock, breech, sights and so on, but there are two main differences between new and old models:

■   The look of the rifles can be very different: the newer model rifles appear to be complex structures and some might even go as far as saying they look more exciting.

■   Almost everything on a newer model will be adjustable. The wooden single-piece rifle is a 'one size fits all' piece of kit, with perhaps some adjustment possible to the butt plates or cheek piece. The newer rifles can be adjusted in many ways, often to within millimetre accuracy.

For a new shooter there is no benefit to be gained from using a newer rifle instead of an older type. The kit has less bearing on the quality of the shooting than the ability of the shooter. Competitors often take part in events with rifles that are many years old and these are just as likely to win as those who have the newest, shiniest rifles.

Ammunition

Shooters attending a first session may find the ammunition is included in the cost of the session, although some clubs may ask for the ammunition to be purchased as an additional cost. Any ammunition that is purchased and not used during the first session must remain at the club because it cannot be removed from the premises.

Small-bore rifle shooting uses a single size of ammunition but there are many different grades and varieties available. The ammunition calibre is .22in (pronounced as 'point two two') and this figure denotes the diameter of the bore (the width of the hole in the barrel). A book intended for advanced shooters could have a whole chapter on how to test and choose ammunition for the best shooting results, but at this early stage the main thing a shooter should be concerned about is how much the ammo costs.

A standard box contains fifty rounds. Ammunition can vary in price depending on the quality. Top grades can cost two or sometimes three times as much per box as the lower grades.

THE RIFLE RANGE: ORIENTATION AND SAFETY

The Rifle Range

Although this is not an item of equipment, the rifle range is a key component to shooting. Just as a footballer must understand the layout of a football pitch, a shooter must know and understand the layout of a rifle range.

Every rifle club will look different and may have different facilities available to the shooters, but each will have a firing range and most have basic WC facilities and a club room. Some may have a club house with a kitchen area and an armoury for keeping club guns. Clubs have even been known to have a fully licensed bar (but only for use *after* shooting!)

Firing range. The area used for the purpose of shooting. At one end there is an area with targets and at the other an area for the shooters (the firing point).

Target area. The targets are set up here and are fixed at a distance from the firing point. (For more information on the type of targets used *see* Chapter Ten.)

Stop butts. The bullets are stopped here; this can be an earth bank (if outdoors) or a metal 'bullet catcher'.

Baffles. Angled or vertical plates of steel often fixed across the width of an indoor range. These prevent any bullets accidentally fired when the rifle was not pointing at the target from leaving the building.

Firing point. The area where shooters position themselves whilst firing. This is directly opposite the targets at a distance of between 15 yards and 100 yards, depending on the type of range. The typical distances are between 15 and 25 yards indoors and 50m/100 yards outdoors.

Firing line. The line marking the edge of the firing point closest to the target and the

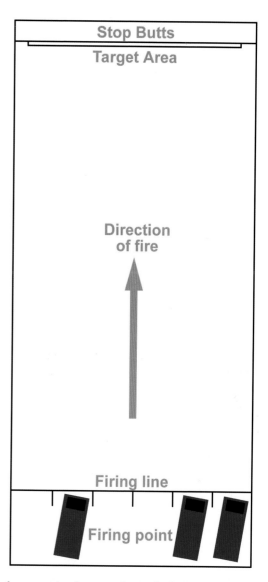

An example of a range layout including most of the items listed in the text.

official mark of the distance from the target to the firing point.

In addition to those listed above, the range may have other features of which shooters should be aware, such as fire escapes, warning signs and range safety lights. These should be pointed out to new shooters on their first visit to the range.

An indoor rifle range viewed from the firing point. There is a clear difference between the firing point and the range area leading towards the target area.

Safety

Shooting is a very safe sport if everyone follows the basic safety rules for handling and using guns or rifles. When visiting a rifle range always be aware of the range safety light, which indicates if the firing range is in use. When the light is on do not enter the range.

Every range has a set of simple rules that must be followed at all times. New starters are not expected to know the rules off by heart, as they will be accompanied at all times during their probationary period by an instructor. The sample set is given here for reference and it is strongly recommended that they are read and observed. Any questions should be raised with the instructor at whichever club the reader attends.

Each club follows a set of standard safety rules and they may have their own rules in addition to those listed here. If you follow these basic rules shooting will be a safe and enjoyable experience. A shooter who fails to follow them may be removed from the range and barred from shooting again at that club or any other in the same region.

Range Safety Rules

The rules given here are an example of range safety rules. The NSRA provides an official set for guidance and these may be presented to the shooter by many clubs when they attend the first shoot.

General Rule

Firearms are only ever safe (unloaded) when they are proven to be empty. Unloaded rifles should always have breech flags inserted that provide visible indications that the rifle is safe.

Specific Rules

1. Only the shooter plus a single instructor may be on a single firing point lane at any one time. Anyone who is watching must stand to the rear of the firing point.
2. Rifles must only be carried or moved when the bolt, or lever, is open and a breech flag is visible in the chamber.
3. Never point a rifle at another person, not even when it is unloaded.
4. Only ever close the bolt when the rifle is pointing down the range towards the target.
5. Rifles are only ever loaded when they are on the firing point and aiming down the range towards the targets or stop butts. A rifle cannot be removed from the firing point when loaded. Permission to load must also have been given by the range officer.
6. On rare occasions rounds may not fire when the trigger has been squeezed. This is known as a misfire. If a misfire occurs the rifle should be unloaded carefully, and the misfired round given to the range conducting officer to dispose of safely.
7. Never remove a loaded rifle from the firing point and always unload the rifle before getting up from the firing point. Even if the shooter is only moving a short distance away from the rifle it should be unloaded and a breech flag inserted.
8. Never go in front of a person who is shooting. No one may move towards the targets unless the range officer has said the range is clear and people may move forwards. If there is a problem with a target during the shoot the range officer should be notified.
9. If the range officer says STOP then everyone must stop firing, unload, and insert a breech flag. Further instructions will be given by the range officer.

Personal Safety

Every time a rifle is fired a loud noise is made. This 'crack' can permanently damage the hearing of anyone in close proximity, and no one is closer to the noise than the person firing the rifle.

Ear plugs can be used as ear protection. These are not usually suitable for younger shooters as they can be difficult to fit properly. Ear defenders should be used instead.

Ear defenders should cover the whole ear and conform to the current EU safety standards.

Clubs providing opportunities for people to learn to shoot must ensure hearing protection of sufficient quality is made available. Hearing protection takes the form of ear defenders or ear plugs. It is important that the quality of the equipment is sufficient: if the equipment provided appears to be damaged, does not fit or is in any way unsuitable it must be raised with the instructor prior to the start of firing.

For shooters under the age of eighteen the rifle club can be held accountable for damage to hearing caused by shooting if suitable protection is not provided. Therefore, clubs must provide hearing protection of the required standard and ensure it is worn by the shooter at the correct times.

Adults must be provided with the correct equipment, but are liable for their own decision to wear it or not.

As with many sports, the shooter is advised to be aware that if they have any concerns about eye safety then eye protection can be worn without detrimental effect to the ability to shoot.

A shooter should be aware that handling firearms and ammunition will leave a residue of oils, lead and other chemicals on their hands, which should be washed properly at the end of the session or before eating.

SETTING UP AND USING A RIFLE

Firing Point Set-Up

As a general rule the firing point should be free of clutter. It should contain the rifle with a breech flag, a mat, an ammo block (optional) and the supporting stand or sandbag for the rifle.

The instructor may have a scope so that the shots fired can be seen on the target. This is not to see how well the shooter is doing, it should be used only to check that the shots are hitting the correct target. If the new shooter hits anything other than the target (for example, the floor, ceiling, walls or another target) the instructor can pause the session and attempt to find out and correct whatever is causing the shots to miss.

A typical firing point set-up with the rifle already in place. A mat, rifle stand and an ammunition block are also visible.

The rifle must always point down the range towards the target. If the firing point is set up before the new shooter arrives the rifle will already be in position on the mat. If the new shooter has been asked to carry the rifle to the firing point it must be placed on the mat with the muzzle pointing down the range.

Rifles should have a breech flag inserted at all times, except when being loaded and fired. The breech flag is a small tag, usually plastic, that is inserted into the breech and shows, even from a distance, that the rifle is not loaded and is safe.

Lying Down with the Rifle

The following list provides a step-by-step guide to lying down with a rifle. When using a rifle for the first time an instructor should be present to provide assistance and guidance. (If the shooter

---

Carrying Rifles

It is not uncommon for new starters to be asked, after receiving a safety briefing, to carry the rifle from the rack to the firing point. This can provide the first hands-on experience of handling a weapon.

When being carried the rifle must always be held pointing upwards and a breech flag should be visible.

Handy Tips

Before shooting it is advisable to empty all items from trouser pockets – lying down on a bunch of keys is not usually very comfortable. If the shooter is wearing a belt with a large buckle it should be removed as they too can be uncomfortable to lie on.

It is also important that mobile phones are switched off. Others at the club may be shooting competition cards and usually do not welcome distractions caused by ring tones and text alerts.

is left-handed, reverse all of the 'right/left' instructions described here.)

■ Stand at the end of the mat facing the target: the mat should be at an angle of 10–20 degrees from the firing line

■ The rifle should be at the end of the mat nearer the target and on the right-hand side.

■ Lie down on the mat with the centre line of the body in line with the centre of the mat. This will put the body at an angle to the target.

■ Pick up the rifle, keeping it pointed down the range, and place the butt in the right shoulder.

■ The weight of the rifle is supported on a stand or a sandbag.

■ The left elbow is extended in front of the shooter's left shoulder, with the hand lightly gripping the underside of the stock about halfway along the length (this will vary with both the length of the stock and the arm).

■ The right hand lightly grips the pistol grip – *do not put a finger on the trigger*.

■ Extend the right elbow out to the right of the body until comfortable (this may support some of the weight of the upper body).

■ Once the arms, elbows and hands are in the right positions, the head can be lowered until the right cheek rests on the cheek piece of the rifle: the right eye should be directly behind the sights and able to see through the small hole in the rear sight.

Common Problems

■ Rifle pointing at ceiling/floor: If the butt is correctly placed in the shoulder, adjust the position of the body forwards or backwards

How to lie with a rifle that is supported on a stand.

The rifle butt is correctly positioned in the shoulder.

The rifle butt is too high in the shoulder.

The rifle butt is too low in the shoulder.

Upper body and arm positions when the rifle is supported on a stand. The index finger should only be on the trigger when firing. At all other times it should rest on the stock.

until the rifle is pointing at the target. If excessive movement is required or the position is uncomfortable, lower or raise the stand/sandbag to level the rifle.

- Rifle pointing to the left or right of the target: adjust body position to the left or right until the rifle points towards the target.
- Left elbow is painful: most clubs will have elbow pads to help cushion the elbows. If no pads are available, fold a jumper or other item of clothing and place it under the affected elbow.
- Sights are touching the face or are too far away: either the head is pushed too far forwards or the neck is 'scrunched up', relax the neck. If this does not improve the situation the sights might need to be moved: ask the instructor for guidance.
- Eye cannot see through the sights because it doesn't line up properly behind the rear sight: the head may be in the wrong position or the butt may be too high/low in the shoulder. This is one occasion where the sights should not be moved to fix this issue: it is head and body position adjustments that will resolve this.

It is usually quite simple to set up with a supported rifle and, after a bit of shuffling around on the mat, the new shooter should be able to find a comfortable position with the rifle pointing toward the target, while being able to look through the sights.

How to Aim

Many individuals use corrective lenses to improve their vision. Positioning the head behind the sights while wearing glasses is possible and it should not interfere with the shooter's ability to aim properly. If the shooter finds this awkward or uncomfortable, specialist shooting glasses fitted with prescription lenses can be purchased.

Aiming with a rifle involves lining up three separate points: a pair of sights (a rear sight and a foresight) with one at each end of the rifle, and the target as the third aiming point. If this is done accurately the shooter will be able to hit the target when the shot is fired – simple.

Different types of sight are used on rifles. Each does the same thing by aiding the shooter to aim the rifle, but in a different way. The most

Different sight pictures are created by the different types of rifle sights. These diagrams show what is seen when both the fore- and rear sight are aligned correctly.

common sights for small-bore rifles are circular sights, but shooters may also come across blade and notch sights.

In the diagrams above the images show the 'perfect' sight picture, with each element of the image having well-defined edges. The reality is a little different because the eye cannot clearly focus on objects at different distances at the same time.

When aiming, the rear sight will never be well defined or clear because it is positioned too close to the eye and the eye cannot focus on objects closer than 15cm (6in).

The foresight is about 100cm away from the eye and the target is 25 yards away (depending on the length of the range). Both of these can easily be focused independently. What the eye cannot do is focus on both the foresight and the target at the same time.

The shooter should focus on the foresight instead of the target. In this case the target should appear as a slightly blurred spot and the eye will automatically try to make the shooter line up the target and the foresight. If the eye focuses on the target the foresight becomes blurry and it is much harder to align the target and the sights, thus making it harder to shoot accurately.

Loading

Although loading takes place before aiming in the firing process, it has been inserted here after

ABOVE: *The actual view through the rear sight with the eye focusing on the foresight. The foresight is clearly defined and the target appears as a slightly blurred spot.*

BELOW: *The view through the rear sight with the eye focusing on the target. The target appears to be well defined and the foresight is blurry.*

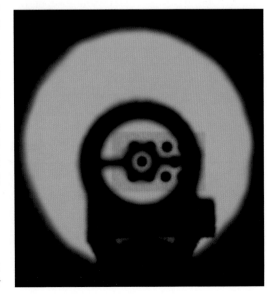

the aiming section so that the basics of aiming are understood and can be practised before the rifle is loaded. When the rifle is loaded it is better if the shooter already knows how to aim it at the target, rather than be unsure of how to aim while holding a 'live' weapon.

During the first session the loading will almost certainly be done by the instructor. This allows the shooter to focus on shooting at the target and not to worry about anything else. If the shooter is allowed to load, the instructor will demonstrate the following steps:

- Keep the rifle pointed down the range (towards the target) at all times.
- Remove the breech flag from the rifle.
- Pick up a round, holding it by the rim at the flat end of the brass case.
- Place the front of the round at the mouth of the breech.
- Gently push the round forward with a finger (or thumb) until it is fully inserted into the breech.
- Make sure the rifle is still pointing down the range.

Hold the round by the end of the brass case when putting it into the breech.

Use the thumb (or a finger) to push the round all the way into the chamber before closing the bolt.

■ Slide the bolt forward and push the bolt handle down until the bolt is fully closed (or close the lever for Martini actions).

At this point the rifle is loaded, cocked and ready to fire. If there is a problem for any reason the shooter must immediately ask for help from the instructor and keep their finger away from the trigger. If the instructor is unavailable, place the rifle on the ground with the muzzle pointing down the range towards the target and move back away from the rifle to wait for the instructor.

FIRING THE FIRST SHOTS

With the rifle loaded the shooter should aim at the target and, when they are satisfied the sight picture is correct, they should gently squeeze the trigger until the shot is fired.

There are a number of valid questions commonly asked about what happens when the first shot is fired: Will it be really loud? Does the rifle move very much? Will it bang into my shoulder? Will the sights hit me in the face? To prepare the shooter for the first shot, here is a brief description of what will happen.

The shooter is lying down correctly, the rifle is loaded and aimed properly and it is now time to squeeze the trigger … squeeze, squeeze … BANG!!

That is really all there is to it. The rifle will make a loud crack when it is fired, although this noise will be negligible when the proper hearing protection is worn. The rifle will move no more than a few millimetres and there is no big 'thud' into the shoulder. If the head is correctly aligned behind the sights, nothing will touch the face when a round is fired. If the sights are very close to the eye they can usually be moved forward to provide a larger gap.

On completion of the firing session it is important that the shooter collects all empty cases from the firing point and places them in an

---

Handy Tip

If some shots have missed the target altogether, the reader should check that they are looking through the rear sight and not over or around it – the sight picture should look similar to that shown in the section on p.29 about aiming.

---

appropriate container for disposal or recycling. Empty cases must not be removed from the range and they should not be kept as souvenirs.

What to Expect from the First Shots

When learning to shoot it is not important how close the holes are to the centre of the target. Instead look for how close the holes are to each other. This is called 'group size'. Group size is a key measure of a shooter's ability and a good method for tracking progress.

The group size of any new shooter will vary depending on their level of knowledge, clarity of eyesight and general shooting aptitude. If the shooter has a basic understanding of how to use both the sights and trigger before taking their first shots, the chances of a reasonable group will be much better.

For every new shooter the first shots taken should appear on the target area, which here means anywhere on the cardboard target. There is only a problem if the holes are either missing or they appear in the frame holding the target.

It is not the place of the author to say what is good or bad from a first shoot. Everybody has their own level of ability and will start out with different group sizes.

FIRST TIME SHOOTING: DOS AND DON'TS

■ Do listen to the safety briefing given at the start of the session.

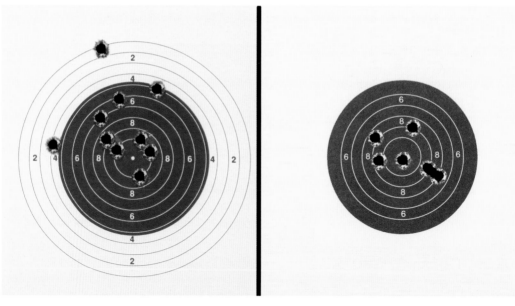

Group sizes will vary the first time someone uses a rifle. Accuracy will improve with time and practice. Note that not all groups are in the centre of the target.

■ Do wear ear protection of a suitable standard.

■ Do make sure a breech flag is used at all times when the rifle is not being loaded or fired.

■ Do ask questions if there is anything that is not clear.

■ Do empty pockets before lying down to shoot.

■ Do ensure lying down behind the rifle is comfortable: elbow pads or something soft can make a big difference in the level of comfort.

■ Do make sure the eye is looking through the rear sight and that the foresight is in the centre of the rear sight aperture.

■ And remember that if there is a problem of any kind, move away from the rifle and get the attention of the instructor in a safe way.

■ Do not break any of the safety rules.

■ Do not take a mobile phone onto the firing point.

■ Do not point the rifle anywhere other than down the range towards the target.

■ Do not tense when taking a shot.

■ Do not close the eyes while firing a shot – they need to be open to make sure the rifle is pointing at the target.

Above all just enjoy it.

CHAPTER 4

SHOOTING WITH A SUPPORTED RIFLE

This chapter builds on the theory from Chapter Three and provides simple exercises that enable a new shooter to practise and track progress in the key skill areas of breathing, aiming, trigger control and follow through. Following these exercises will guide the reader into good habits that will help with future development.

By the end of this chapter the shooter should be able to set up their firing point, feel confident when loading, aiming and firing, and be able to shoot a group size of 1 inch or less with a supported rifle.

Some people will take only an hour of shoot-ing to achieve these goals, while others might take ten hours or maybe longer. It is important to remember that each person develops skills and learns new things at a different rate and that taking time over learning to shoot is no bad thing.

SHOOTING FOR THE SECOND TIME

The first time a person shoots is not the best time for an in-depth discussion on complex shooting techniques. Most likely they will be

Shooting with the rifle supported on a stand.

focusing on what it is like to fire a gun for the first time or perhaps how long it might take to become an Olympic shooting champion. They will be a lot less likely to be thinking about (or interested in) the perfect breathing rhythm and smooth trigger action combination for a well-aimed shot. Once the first shots have been fired, the targets examined and the congratulations (or lamentations) are delivered, it is then the right time to start learning the proper techniques of shooting.

Small-bore rifle shooting is a sport in which the key skill is the ability to reproduce the exact same set of actions each and every time a shot is fired. Numerous different things can affect where the shot hits the target, and each has a different magnitude of effect on the shot. The best thing to do is to first learn the core skills that have the greatest effect on the shot. Once those have been mastered the remaining topics can be covered one by one.

For small-bore shooting with a supported rifle there are four core skills: breathing rhythm, sight picture (aiming), trigger control and follow through.

DEVELOPING CORE SKILLS: BREATHING

Breathing is the most natural thing for a person to do and each person usually breathes without any conscious thought. The human body also adapts the way it breathes to suit different situations. For example, breathing becomes fast and deep when the body is physically exerting itself and is slow and shallow when at rest. Breathing will unconsciously change to match any activity the body engages in. However, some activities require that breathing is paused for a few moments. This might be because the person is unable to breath owing to the location, perhaps swimming underwater, or because breathing prevents one from being perfectly still for a short period of time. The need to be motionless in the

final moments of aiming and firing a shot requires a conscious control of breathing by the shooter.

How Breathing Affects the Body and the Shot

When breathing your chest expands and if you are lying flat on your stomach each breath taken raises the body up off the ground a little bit. If someone is lying down when holding a rifle the breathing motion will be transferred to the rifle – and the task of aiming precisely is made a lot more difficult with a moving rifle. This is why, for a few seconds while aiming and firing a shot, the shooter must hold their breath. To minimize movement in the rifle when breathing, the shooter should raise the right knee (for a right-handed shooter) as this has the effect of raising the diaphragm, allowing for expansion and contraction of the lungs without the body lifting significantly up and down.

Do not hold a breath for too long. After about 5 seconds the oxygen levels in the blood start to reduce and this will have an immediate effect on the shooter's vision. If a breath is held in the lungs for too long then physiological effects begin to occur as the level of oxygen in the lungs becomes insufficient to meet the needs of the body. These effects will have an impact on the shooter's ability to focus accurately on the rifle sights and the target.

How Much Air Should Be in the Lungs When Holding Your Breath?

The commonly used phrase for the amount of air a person should hold in their lungs while taking a shot is to have the lungs 'half full'. The reason why holding a breath with either full or empty lungs is not a good idea can be demonstrated in a simple exercise (but do not try this exercise less than 30 minutes before shooting because it will have a negative impact on aiming).

Take a deep breath and hold it for about 20 seconds. At the end of this time think about the physical and mental experience you have just had. Common experiences are:

■ The mind is thinking about the breath being held for as long as possible and this distracts from other tasks such as aiming.
■ The body experiences discomfort as the diaphragm attempts to push upwards and expel the air from the lungs. This causes a 'straining' sensation at the base of the lungs.
■ After the person has released the breath they immediately take another deep breath to help raise the oxygen levels in the blood and for a few seconds the body's whole focus is on breathing.

In the next part of the exercise, breathe all the way out, empty the lungs, and then stay like this for about 20 seconds. The common effects of this are very similar to the previous experience of holding a full breath:

■ The body will try to breathe in, thus forcing the person to focus on not breathing. This makes it difficult for the mind to focus on anything else.
■ Discomfort as the diaphragm tries to draw breath into the lungs.
■ As soon as it is allowed to breathe again the body's main focus is on getting air into the lungs and expelling the build-up of CO_2 in the blood.

The exercise just described shows the physical effects of holding too much or too little breath in the lungs. There is an additional effect that also impacts the shooter. A simple task might normally take 15 seconds to complete, but if the same person is asked to complete the same task while holding their breath, they will try to complete the task more quickly and this will likely lead to mistakes being made.

When firing a shot the shooter needs to remain focused and relaxed throughout. Anything that caused them to rush or lose focus will prevent the shot from being as good as it could be.

Lungs Half Full

There are two difficulties with trying to get the lungs half full. One is that the human body does not have a gauge that shows how full the lungs are, so there is no easy way of telling if the lungs are a third, half or three-fifths full, or any other amount. The other difficulty is that each shot taken should be with the same amount of air in the lungs. Since we are not able to tell how much air is in the lungs even once, trying to get the same unknown volume of air exactly right for every shot appears to be impossible.

Fortunately, shooters have a visible indicator to show how full the lungs are and it is a fairly accurate measure: the sight picture.

When the supported rifle is aiming directly at the target breathing will have a visible effect on the sight picture. In order to see the effect of breathing it is important that the shooter is lying comfortably behind the rifle and is naturally pointing at the target. The target should appear in roughly the centre of the foresight without the shooter having to physically strain to hold the rifle in position. As each breath is taken the rifle will pivot around the point at which it is supported by the stand or sandbag. This pivoting can be seen as the sight picture will appear to move up and down in relation to the target. As the lungs fill with air, the butt of the rifle, which is touching the shoulder, will rise as the body rises off the ground. This causes the muzzle to angle down and the sight picture will be aiming low on the target. Similarly, as the lungs empty the butt of the rifle will drop, causing the rifle to angle upwards and the sight picture will be aiming high on the target.

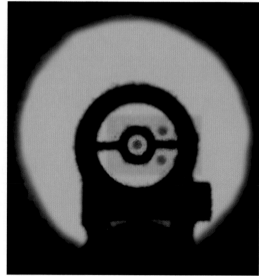

ABOVE: *Sight picture with lungs half full. The target should appear in the centre of the foresight.*

TOP LEFT: *Sight picture with lungs full. When breathing in the rifle will tilt downwards and the target will appear to 'rise'. The aim is low when the lungs are full.*

LEFT: *Sight picture with lungs empty. As the lungs empty the rifle will tilt upwards and the target will 'lower' in the sight picture.*

When the sight picture changes with each breath the point at which the target is in the centre of the foresight indicates when the lungs are half full.

Handy Tip

If the target is in the centre of the foresight when the lungs are either full or empty, the body position should be moved forward or backward so that the target is in the centre of the foresight, midway between full and empty lungs.

Handy Tip

Always fire the shot after breathing all the way in and halfway out. If the breath is held while breathing in, the body will have less oxygen in the blood and the duration that the shooter is able to hold their breath will be greatly reduced. Always hold halfway through the outward breath.

If the general body position does not move between shots then the shooter has a visual gauge of how full the lungs are for every shot they take.

DEVELOPING CORE SKILLS: SIGHT PICTURE AND AIMING

The term 'sight picture' refers to what is seen when the shooter looks through the rear sight. The picture comprises the different elements of the rifles' sights and the target, with the sight picture being either good or bad. The basics of how to aim are covered in Chapter Three and the information given there will help the reader understand the following section.

The correct sight picture is gained by focusing on the foresight, ensuring that the foresight is visible in the centre of the rear sight and lining up the slightly blurry target in the centre of the foresight before taking the shot. This is the very basic method for aiming and should result in the shot hitting the black area of the target. By itself, however, this will not be enough to shoot a consistent group of shots that all hit the target very close together.

To achieve a tight group the three elements of the sight picture must be perfectly aligned. The target and foresight are relatively easy to align when the rifle is supported, since the rifle and therefore the sights do not move very much and can be seen quite clearly. Aligning the foresight in the centre of the rear sight is a little harder. The rear sight of a rifle should not be more than 10cm away from the eye (5–7cm is recommended) and the human eye cannot focus clearly on something that is closer than 15cm (8–10cm for healthy young eyes). In addition, the hole in the centre of the rear sight is roughly 1mm in diameter and the eye must focus through this hole in order to see the foresight. The result of this focus is that the rear sight appears as a blurry black circular hole and does not have a crisp clean edge.

ABOVE: *The perfect sight picture with all elements shown clearly in focus with crisp edges: the barrel and foresight block can be seen breaking the circle of white in the lower portion of the image.*

BELOW: *View through the rear sight. The rear sight edge appears slightly blurred as it is too close to the eye for clear focus.*

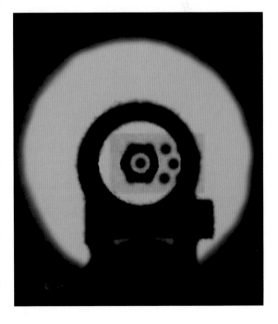

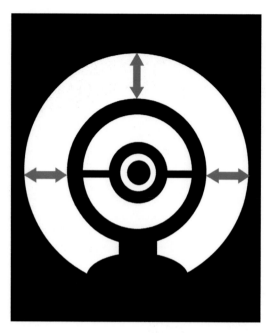

The amount of visible light around the edge of the foresight should be equal all the way around. Light cannot be seen at the bottom of the foresight because the barrel blocks the light.

For the correct sight picture the target and foresight must both be aligned with the rear sight. This means the foresight must appear in the centre of the rear sight with the target showing in the middle of the foresight.

A helpful tip for aligning the foresight in the very middle of the rear sight is to 'look for an even circle of light around the foresight'. There is one slight flaw: the barrel. The rifle barrel breaks up the circle of light surrounding the foresight and this makes judging the vertical alignment of the sights much harder. The best method for ensuring the foresight is always in the same place in the rear sight, although this can be quite difficult to achieve, is to maintain a consistent head position behind the sights.

There is a method for checking the foresight alignment that can be helpful to shooters of all abilities. When the circular foresight and the circular rear sight are aligned, the distance between the edge of the rear sight and the edge of the foresight should remain constant all around the circle. Therefore, a quick way of checking is to see if the amount of light on each side of the foresight is equal to the amount of light above the foresight. Using this method there is no need to check the gap between the bottom of the rear sight and the bottom of the foresight, because if the sides and top are equal then the circular elements of the sights are aligned properly and the head is correctly positioned behind the rear sight.

DEVELOPING CORE SKILLS: SQUEEZING THE TRIGGER

The trigger should be squeezed when the shooter is happy that the sight picture is correct and the breath is being held with lungs half full. Squeezing the trigger may take only a couple of seconds, but it can have a serious effect on where the shot hits the target and is one of the four core skills for rifle shooting.

Finger Position on the Trigger

Although it may seem insignificant, the position of the index finger on the trigger can make the rifle move and cause a shot to miss as the trigger is squeezed. A finger has a different sensitivity in each location, and some parts of it are better at feeling 'touch' than others. The pad of the finger is quite sensitive, whereas the area around the first joint is less sensitive.

Although it is preferable to have the most sensitive part of the finger in contact with the trigger, it will also depend on how stiff the trigger is, along with the position of the hand and finger in relation to the rifle and trigger. A very sensitive trigger can be easily squeezed with the tip of a finger, but a stiff trigger will need a greater force to move it and this will be easier if the trigger is closer to the first joint.

The tip of the index finger should only be used if the trigger is very light.

The pad of the index finger should be used to squeeze the trigger in almost all cases.

Only when the trigger is very heavy (stiff) should the joint of the finger be used instead of the pad.

Types of Trigger

There are two common types of trigger found on small-bore match rifles:

Single-stage. The pressure applied to the trigger is then immediately applied to the firing pin release mechanism.

Two-stage. There is some 'slack' in the trigger movement, so the trigger can be moved a few millimetres, and sometimes more, before any pressure is applied to the firing pin mechanism. The trigger can be moved within this first stage without any effect on the firing pin and it is the second stage where the pressure on the trigger is transferred to the firing pin.

Modern rifles tend to use two-stage triggers with a sophisticated mechanism of interconnected springs to connect the movement of the trigger into the release of the firing pin. These mechanisms are usually mechanical, with the multiple spring systems used to translate small forces on the trigger into large forces in the firing pin, and it is possible to adjust the trigger sensitivity to suit the user. In recent years some electrically controlled firing mechanisms have been created. The overall principle remains the same whichever type is used.

The rifles available to beginners will probably, as previously stated, be older models. These rifles are unlikely to have a 'hair trigger' or match trigger, as is found on newer rifles. Instead the trigger may feel 'heavy' and will require greater force to squeeze than the 'lighter' match trigger. It is important to get used to the type of trigger fitted, since without understanding the different stages of trigger release the shooter will not be able to release the shot at the correct moment.

Trigger Control and Follow Through

Trigger control is the end-to-end process of squeezing the trigger to fire a shot. The different trigger types each require a different 'trigger action', but whatever the type the action should always be smooth. In this case smooth does not mean slow, but rather a single steady squeeze with a finger that is relaxed. The hand on the pistol grip should not be gripping tightly and should not be used to force the rifle to point in the correct direction because accurate shots will be less likely.

Once the shot has been fired it is important to keep the trigger squeezed for a short period before releasing it. This is called the 'follow through'. If the trigger is released immediately as the shot is fired then the motion of release could move the rifle very slightly, enough to alter the aim and cause the shot to miss the centre of the target.

A common mistake for beginners is to squeeze the trigger too fast and too hard, followed by immediately releasing the trigger. This is often accompanied by a movement of the head away from the sights. The trigger does not

---

Handy Tip

Try 'dry firing' a few times to get used to the trigger pressure on a rifle before firing live rounds. Cock the rifle and gently squeeze the trigger (insert a plastic dry fire plug to prevent damage to the firing pin). The shooter should be trying to feel if there are one or two stages in the trigger.

New shooters often miss the first stage of a two-stage trigger because they are not aware of its existence or they are unused to applying such a light pressure with the tip of a finger. Asking a more experienced shooter can help quickly identify the trigger type being used.

have to be squeezed very hard, as only enough pressure should be applied to fire the shot.

The follow through does not require the trigger to be squeezed as far back as it will move. All that is required is to maintain enough pressure so that it stays in the same position for a couple of seconds.

If smooth, consistent trigger control is applied with a follow through, it can greatly reduce a common cause of shots going wide.

PRACTISE EXERCISES

New shooters have so much theory to remember that it can be difficult to apply all of it at the same time. The exercises in the following pages help to put into practice the theory covered so far, showing the effects of different methods and enabling the shooter to track their development over time for each core skill.

The exercises can be done in any order and as many or as few times as is necessary because it all counts as practise. Each exercise involves firing groups of five shots at the same diagram on a target. Remember that at this stage it does not matter how close to the centre of the target the group appears, it is the size of the group that is important.

It can be useful to have someone watch the shooter while working through an exercise so that any areas for improvement can be highlighted. The instructor or an experienced club member should be able to help as an observer.

Breathing: Half Breaths and Body Position

Format: Shoot three five-shot groups. This exercise requires a target with at least three diagrams.

Core focus: How to recognize when the lungs are half full.

Description: This simple exercise demonstrates the effect of shooting when the lungs are full, empty or half full. It also shows how moving the body on the mat will adjust the centre of the aiming point up or down.

Method for the First Group of Five Shots
Shoot a five-shot group on a single diagram following these steps:

1. Get into the prone position with the rifle pointing at the target.
2. When comfortable the shooter should look through the sights and observe the position of the target in relation to the foresight. When breathing normally the motion of the target should rise and fall through the centre of the foresight. This motion, as well as the position of the highest and lowest points of the cycle, should be noted.
3. Adjust the position of the body until the highest point of the foresight motion is the point where the target is in the centre of the foresight. This will be when the lungs are almost empty.
4. Keeping the body in the same position, the five-shot group should be fired.

Method for the Second Group of Five Shots
For the second of the five-shot groups the shooter should repeat the steps as for the first group, but replace step 3 with the following:

3. Adjust the position of the body backwards (away from the target) until the lowest point of the foresight motion is the point where the target is in the centre of the foresight. This will be when the lungs are almost full.

Method for the Third Group of Five Shots
For the third of the five-shot groups the shooter should repeat the steps as for the first group, but replace step 3 with the following:

3. Adjust the position of the body until the highest and lowest points of the foresight motion appear the same distance above and below the target. The point at which the target is in the centre of the foresight is when the lungs are half full.

Usual result: The first two group sizes should be roughly the same, and the third group should be visibly smaller than either of the first two.

Sight Picture: Foresight and Target Focus

Format: Shoot two five-shot groups on different diagrams on a single target.
Core focus: Where the eye should be focusing in the sight picture.
Description: This exercise highlights the effect on grouping if the shooter focuses on the foresight element or on the target. Shoot a group while focusing on the foresight and shoot a separate group on a clean diagram focusing on the target instead of the foresight.

Method
Shoot a five-shot group on a single diagram following these steps:

1. Get into the prone position with the rifle pointing at the target.
2. When the position is correctly aligned the shooter should load and prepare to fire the shot.
3. While aiming, the eye should be focused on the foresight element. The foresight should be visible with crisp edges and the target should be a slightly 'fuzzy' spot in the centre of the foresight.
4. Fire each of the five shots with the focus on the foresight.

Shoot the second five-shot group on a clean diagram using the same method as before, but replace step 4 with this:

4. While aiming the eye should be focused on the target and not on the foresight element. The foresight should be visible as a slightly blurry circle surrounding the clearly visible black spot that is the target.

In each grouping exercise the shooter should be thinking about the position of the foresight as seen through the rear sight. If there is an even amount of white around the foresight it indicates that the foresight is in line with the centre of the rear sight.

Usual result: The size of the group will usually be smaller when the eye focuses on the foresight rather than on the target.

Trigger Control

Format: Shoot a five-shot group on a single diagram.
Core focus: Smooth and steady trigger control.
Description: This exercise helps a shooter practise a smooth and steady trigger control for each shot fired. The shooter should consciously be thinking about gently squeezing the trigger and ensuring a good follow through for every shot.

Method
Shoot a five-shot group on a single diagram following these steps:

1. Get into the prone position with the rifle pointing at the target.
2. When the position is correctly aligned the shooter should load and prepare to fire the shot.
3. Breathing should remain steady and natural while the sight picture is aligned.

4. When the sight picture is correctly aligned, hold the breath (lungs half full).
5. Gently squeeze the trigger, taking up the first stage if using a two-stage trigger.
6. Squeeze through the pressure and fire the shot, remembering to keep the pressure on the trigger and ensure at least a 2 second follow through is held.
7. Repeat the process for each of the four remaining shots in the group.

After the exercise is finished the shooter should think back on the shots fired and highlight any that were taken with a rushed or jerky trigger action. It is nothing to be ashamed of if any of the shots were taken without a smooth trigger action, but it is something to work on improving.

MOVING ON TO THE NEXT STAGE

Up to this point the shooting has been done with the butt of the rifle held in the shoulder but with the weight of the rifle supported on a stand or a sandbag. Supporting the weight of the rifle enables the shooter to focus on the core skills of breathing, sight picture, trigger control and follow through while maintaining a fairly stable position.

To progress further the shooter must be able to support the rifle using a jacket and sling instead of a stand. This is probably the most challenging step taken by new shooters, since the weight and balance of the rifle will be provided by an outstretched arm rather than on a solid stand or sandbag.

Before attempting the challenges raised by the removal of the fixed rifle support, it is important for the shooter to have reasonable ability in each of the core skills. If a shooter has trouble getting a consistent group while using a stand then they will find it almost impossible to shoot a good group without it.

For this reason it is important for the new shooter to practise the core skills with a supported rifle until they can shoot a group that is on average 15mm in diameter. Once the shooter is confident that they can maintain this level of consistency then it is time to move

---

Why Shoot Groups of Five Shots Instead of Ten?

Most of the practice exercises included here are based on shooting groups of five shots at a single diagram. The exercises could be done with ten-shot groups instead, but there are a few reasons why five shots might be preferable:

- Five shots may not be enough to show the full size of a shooter's group, but it does give an indication whether the group is 5cm wide or just 1cm wide.
- Shooting a large number of rounds can be tiring for people new to the sport. For exercises requiring multiple groups to be shot, firing fifteen shots or thirty shots can make a big difference to the shooter's level of comfort.
- If the shooter becomes physically tired or uncomfortable during the exercise, the quality of their shooting will reduce and distort the outcome of the exercise as errors begin to occur.
- Each exercise requires the shooter to think back on what they have done after they finish shooting. If ten shots have been fired it can be difficult to remember each one individually and recall whether the focus was believed to be correct or not for each shot. Five shots is a small enough number for the shooter to remember, for example, that the second shot went 'a bit to the right'.

forward to using a jacket and sling. Trying to remove the stand before this level of consistency is reached can lead to frustration as group sizes will be much less consistent and progress will be very slow.

SECOND TIME SHOOTING: DOS AND DON'TS

- Do continue to be safe and obey safety and range rules.
- Do wear ear protection of a suitable standard.
- Do ask questions if there is anything that is not clear.
- Do be prepared for improvement to happen in stages over time.
- Do mix and match the shooting exercises, try new things and note their effect on the group size.
- Do remember it is about group size and not how close the group is to the centre of the target. This can be adjusted at a later stage.
- Do not rush through the exercises. Shooting is about precision and it cannot be rushed.
- Do not take too long either. If something looks and feels right then take the shot. Procrastinating is almost as bad as rushing.
- Do not feel pressured into moving onto the jacket and sling stage too soon. Ensure key skills are being achieved at a reasonable level before attempting to move on.

CHAPTER 5

SHOOTING WITH A JACKET AND SLING

The progression from shooting with a rifle supported on a stand to shooting with the weight of the rifle held by the shooter is a large step to take, but not difficult. This chapter covers the equipment that will be used and some of the more common methods and techniques for setting up a good prone position. At this stage the shooter will almost certainly still be a probationary member of the club and should be looking to use club equipment for their prone shooting.

When making the transition to holding the rifle without a stand the shooter should be aware that their group size may become larger. It is important to remember that this is not a backward step but is progression, with a new technique to be mastered, and although it may take some time to get used to, it will ultimately lead to much smaller group sizes.

The quality of the prone position a shooter uses has a noticeable effect on the quality of their shooting. With the weight of the rifle supported on a stand or sandbag, the body position in relation to the rifle and target will have only a minor effect on the outcome of each shot. When the stand is removed it is

A shooter using a jacket and sling to support the rifle instead of a stand or a sandbag.

now the shooter's body that must support the rifle and provide a stable platform with almost no movement. In this case the position of the body in relation to the rifle and target has a notable effect on the outcome of each shot.

Everybody has a different shape and size. These differences mean that there is no such thing as 'one position fits all'. This chapter will help newcomers to the sport to find the position that is right for them.

THE KIT

The most obvious piece of kit used by a shooter is the rifle, which has been described in some detail in the Chapter Two. This section covers how to select the rifle that is the correct size for the shooter.

Three items a shooter should have in addition to a rifle are a jacket, sling and glove, each of which need to be of the correct size. A shooting mat can also be added to this list, as it makes

Checking rifle stock length using the arm. This rifle is too short as the index finger extends beyond the trigger even with the wrist bent.

This rifle is too long as the index finger cannot reach the trigger.

the ground a lot more comfortable. As with rifles, there is a wide range of age, type and quality of kit that may be encountered.

The quality of kit can be very important at the top levels of competition but at the entry level the kit quality usually only affects the aesthetics: it may look a bit tatty but it still does the job.

The Rifle

Rifles are available in a range of sizes. Using a rifle that is the wrong size will prevent the shooter from building a good prone position and may also be uncomfortable. If any progress is going to be made towards shooting without a stand it is important to ensure the new shooter is using a rifle of the correct size.

Two important factors for a rifle are the weight and the length of the stock. If the rifle is too big or heavy the shooter may not be able to hold the weight over a period of more than a few minutes. If the stock is too long (or short) it can be difficult to align the eye correctly with the sights.

There is a simple 'rule of thumb' method used to check if a rifle is the correct size for the shooter. Holding the rifle vertically, the butt is placed against the upper arm as close to the elbow joint as possible. The hand should be able to wrap around the pistol grip comfortably.

This rifle is the correct size as the index finger comfortably reaches the trigger.

Keeping a Notebook

Keeping good records of the kit used will ensure the same rifle, jacket and sling are used in each shooting session. When kit is borrowed from a club it is likely to be shared by a number of shooters and each person will have a different prone position and therefore different settings on the equipment they use. Each shooter should keep a personal log of the kit they are using and how it is set up.

If the fingers cannot easily reach the trigger, or if most of the hand is above the grip, then the rifle is the wrong size.

Some rifles can be adjusted to change the length of the stock and increase the distance between the trigger and the butt plate. If this is available then the rifle stock can be adjusted to get the right length for the shooter. If the stock is not adjustable, the shooter should try to use a rifle that is a good fit, there may not be a rifle that is perfect for each shooter but a 'close fit' should be fine at this stage.

Jackets are available in many styles and sizes. Clubs usually have older or more basic kit available to borrow.

Jackets

The core purpose of a shooting jacket is to provide a fixed position on the arm of the shooter to which the sling can be attached. This is usually achieved by having a 'hook' fixed near the top of the arm on the jacket. There are additional benefits provided by jackets, such as padding in the elbows to make supporting the weight of the rifle more comfortable while lying down. Jackets also provide bracing across the shoulders to help with the stability and repeatability (more on this later) of the prone position. What a jacket does not do is replace the skeletal support and muscular control required to hold the rifle. Good kit can help a person support a rifle, but the core support must come from their body position.

Older jackets are usually made from single-thickness fabric whereas modern jackets have the option of single- or double-thickness canvas, leather or synthetic materials. Sections of the jacket may have a non-slip material attached to help prevent the butt of the rifle moving in the shoulder or to stop the elbows from slipping on the mat. Despite more expensive jackets being adjustable and using sections made from different materials, they are not very different from older jackets and provide many of the same basic benefits.

Handy Tip

A new shooter should learn the principles and skills of shooting before purchasing or using high-quality kit. The kit can improve the shooter a little bit, but only if the core skills have been learnt and well practised.

Jackets should not fit like a normal suit jacket. A shooting jacket should be snug, but not uncomfortably tight. A basic way to test the fit of a jacket is for the wearer to try to touch their elbows together in front of their body. (This should be done gently so that neither the jacket nor the wearer is damaged.) The elbows should get no closer than about 200mm: if they touch then the jacket is too big, and if the jacket is uncomfortable then it might be too small.

It is recommended that something like a long-sleeved T-shirt and a sweatshirt are worn under the jacket as this will provide greater comfort and additional padding for the elbows. The sweatshirt should not be too baggy as this can cause the clothing to bunch up uncomfortably inside the sleeves. It is also recommended to wear the same clothing at each shooting session to ensure consistency.

Slings

The sling is a vital piece of equipment for the prone shooter. When lying down the shooter must support the entire weight of the rifle, with almost all of the weight supported by the left arm (for a right-handed person), which is

ABOVE: *The elbows touching shows this jacket is too large.*

BELOW LEFT: *If the elbows are not touching and are less than shoulder width apart the jacket is a reasonable fit.*

BELOW RIGHT: *The elbows cannot touch and are far apart, which shows the jacket is too small. Not being able to do up the buttons (or zip) also indicate the jacket is too small.*

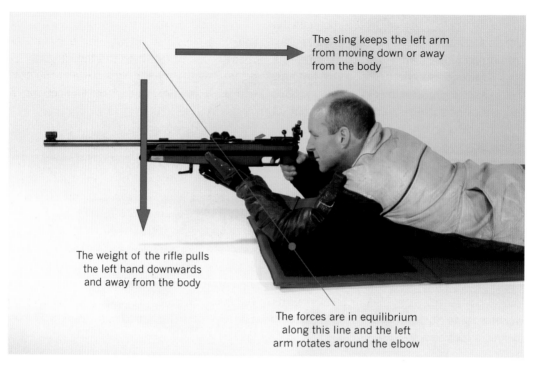

The sling keeps the left arm from moving down or away from the body

The weight of the rifle pulls the left hand downwards and away from the body

The forces are in equilibrium along this line and the left arm rotates around the elbow

ABOVE: *The sling holds the left arm up and allows the muscles in the arm to relax.*

BELOW: *Slings are available in leather or plastic. Some have more holes for adjusting the length than others, therefore allowing for more accurate adjustment.*

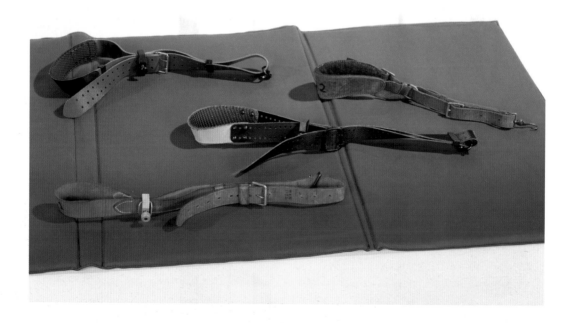

stretched out in front of the shooter. Without a sling, the muscles in the left arm must hold the rifle in position, but with a sling, the weight of the rifle is transferred to the skeleton, allowing the muscles in the arm to relax.

There are different types of sling but they all perform the same function – helping support the weight of the rifle and steadying the position of the shooter. Slings are made from leather or plastic, with only a couple of differences between the two.

Leather slings can stretch a little during use, which can make it harder to get the correct tension in the sling, whereas plastic slings do not stretch, but they can be more difficult to adjust because they are stiff. Some slings may have a 'tension' adjuster included, which allows the shooter to adjust the sling while remaining in position with the rifle.

Slings are available in different lengths and can be adjusted to fit the arm length of the shooter. The correct length of the sling will be determined when first setting up the prone position and can be changed as the position is developed over time.

If the shooter is right handed the sling is worn high on the left arm, and will be located in the sling hook attached to the jacket.

The sling is shaped to fit comfortably around the upper arm with the top of the arm loop being wider than the bottom, although this may be difficult to see if the sling is old because it may have changed shape after many years of use. When the sling is fitted it will extend out from the arm. The buckle for adjusting the length of the sling should always be situated on the side nearest to the body, so making it easier to adjust.

Slings should be positioned high on the upper arm. They are usually held in place with buckles or hooks that are attached to the jacket.

ABOVE: The sling should not be too far away from the body.

TOP LEFT: Slings should not be too close to the body.

LEFT: The sling should extend away from the arm so that it pulls evenly from both sides when attached to the rifle.

Gloves

For right-handed shooters the glove is worn on the left hand and is used to provide padding to make supporting the rifle more comfortable and also a non-slip surface for the rifle to sit on. For those who shoot outdoors in winter, and in some indoor ranges too, a glove has the additional benefit of keeping the left hand warm.

Examples of different glove styles: (left) open-fingered mitts; (right) higher quality gloves.

Gloves vary in both material and style, but they all provide the same basic function.

Using a glove that fits properly is very important. The glove should not be too tight or too loose. The section of the glove where the base of the fingers joins should not be touching the webbed part of the hand between the fingers, as this will become uncomfortable while shooting.

There should also be a gap between the tip of each finger and the end of the fingers of the glove. If the glove is too tight it will pinch the skin and restrict circulation, which can result in pins and needles. If the glove is too loose it can move independently of the hand and this can affect the position of the rifle on the palm.

Shooting Mat

This is generally purpose-made for shooting and comprises a lightly padded mat for comfort with a rubberized section on which to place the elbows, to stop them sliding. A shooting mat makes the ground a lot more comfortable to lie on and provides the starting point for building a repeatable prone position, but it does not need to be fitted to the individual shooter.

Handy Tip

Shooting kit should not be uncomfortable. Ill-fitting or uncomfortable kit can be distracting and the shooting will not be as good as it could be.

Aligning the Shooting Mat

It is important that the shooter records the alignment of the mat to the target, for example 15 degrees, as it is this simple step that helps build a robust position.

THE PRONE POSITION

A new shooter might be forgiven for wondering how hard it can be to lie on the ground and hold a rifle. Lying down, pointing a rifle at a target and squeezing the trigger sounds like an easy thing to do. In reality, the position of the body in relation to the rifle, and to the target, takes a lot of work to get right and has a great effect on the quality of the shooting.

As an example of the importance of body position, the shooter should bear in mind that they are trying to hit the very centre of a target that is somewhere between 15 yards and 100 yards away. The width of the centre of the target is so narrow that a small movement can result in missing the centre ring. For example, a 0.25mm movement in the position of the shooter becomes a 6mm movement at the target at 25 yards; this is enough to drop two points out of a possible ten on a single shot. Trying to hold anything steady within a tolerance of 0.25mm using the muscles in the arms is a difficult task. This is why the position and alignment of the body in relation to the target is very important.

There are three common variables in the prone shooting position: the angle at which the body is turned away from the line of fire; the position of the legs in relation to the line of the body; and how far off the ground the torso is raised (upper body and arm placement). Varying the position of each of these has different advantages and the shooter must find, through practise, the combination that suits them best.

The descriptions given in this chapter are for right-handed shooters. If the reader is left handed, the instructions should be changed from left to right and visa versa.

Body Angle Away from the Line of Fire

The torso of the shooter should be lying at an angle of 10–20 degrees from the line of fire. Lying at an angle makes it easier to hold the rifle and it is also easier to position the eye behind the rear sight. Breathing is easier and tension in the neck is reduced. It can sometimes be beneficial to lean the body slightly to the left side as this will improve the range of motion the chest can have while breathing. However, doing this

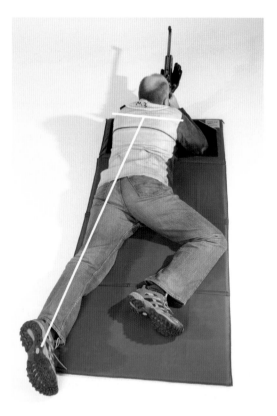

A good basic prone position. The shooter's body is at an angle of 10–20 degrees to the line of fire. Note that the line of the body and shoulders creates a 'T' shape.

TOP LEFT: *The prone position with both legs straight can be more comfortable for some people. The feet are pointing outwards, helping prevent the body from rolling to either side.*

TOP RIGHT: *The prone position with right knee raised toward the torso.*

BELOW RIGHT: *The right knee has been raised too high and is likely to cause discomfort in the back and legs.*

will increase the load in the left arm and it will tire more quickly.

Leg Positions

The left leg of the shooter should extend straight out in line with the body. The foot can point to the left or right, or it can be vertical and resting on the toes. The leg should be relaxed and have no muscle tension.

The right leg position can vary depending on the shooter's preference; it can be extended straight or bent at the knee with the knee drawn up towards the torso. If the leg is straight it should be angled to the right with the foot pointing outwards, away from the body. The angle provides lateral stability to the position and can prevent the shooter from rolling to the left or right.

It is more common for the right leg to be bent at the knee, with the knee drawn up towards the torso. The position of the knee and degree of bend is different for each person, but if raised too high the position can become uncomfortable after a short period of time.

Upper Body Position

There are two main positions for the upper body; the high and the low positions. Each has pros and cons and the reader should try both to find which suits them best.

High Position

Both elbows are positioned close to the body and the chest is raised up off the ground.

Advantages: Breathing is easy as the chest is not on the ground. The eye is looking straight out from the head, which reduces the strain on the eye when focusing on the sight picture.

Disadvantages: A lot of pressure is placed on the elbows because they are supporting the weight of the chest, the head and the rifle.

ABOVE: *High position 1. There is a large angle between the ground and the left forearm. Note that the left hand under the stock is close to the trigger.*

BELOW: *High position 2. Right elbow is bent to a small angle and the head is held near vertical.*

RIGHT: *High position 3. The elbows are drawn in close to the body and the torso is raised up off the mat.*

BELOW: *High position 4. Looking down from above, the high position is identifiable by the elbows being drawn in close to the body and the left hand positioned close to the trigger under the stock.*

Low Position

The left elbow is placed further forward of the body and the left hand should be further forward on the stock than for the high position. Moving the left arm forward will lower the rifle and the chest will be closer to the ground, but the angle between the forearm and the ground must be more than 30 degrees. The right elbow will extend away from the body and be less vertical than in the high position.

Advantages: The low position can be more stable than the high position and the pressure on the elbows is reduced because more of the weight of the chest is supported by the ground and not through the arms.

Disadvantages: The head must be angled down to get the eye behind the rear sight and this angles the eye upwards, making it work a little harder to focus on the sights. It can also be more difficult to keep the sling in position high on the upper arm because of the angle of the arm.

Handy Tip

Wrist watches and belts should be removed prior to shooting. The sling will press against the wrist and if the shooter is wearing a watch this could be caught beneath the sling, which is not very comfortable. Likewise, lying on a belt buckle can be uncomfortable and distracting for the shooter.

ABOVE: *Low position 1. There is a small angle between the ground and the left forearm. Note that the left hand under the stock is close to the front of the rifle.*

BELOW: *Low position 2. Right elbow is bent to a large angle and the head is angled forward to get the eye behind the rear sight.*

RIGHT: *Low position 3. The elbows are far apart and the torso close to the level of the mat.*

BELOW: *Low position 4. Looking down from above, the low position is identifiable by the elbows being extended away from the sides of the body and the left hand positioned much further forward of the trigger than in the high position.*

Whichever position is used the shooter should be both comfortable and stable. Trying to force a position to match one of the photos in this book may cause the position to be incorrect and can even be uncomfortable. Remember, each shooter has a different shape and size and the position they adopt must be the right one for them.

Developing a Prone Shooting Position: Step by Step

The first time a person attempts to use a rifle with a jacket and sling they should always be helped by an experienced person or instructor. The firing point should be set up with a mat and a rifle and the shooter should check they have the equipment they need (*see* above).

One way of getting into the prone position with a jacket and sling for the first time is for the shooter to put on the jacket, sling and glove and then stand at the end of the mat facing the target. Bending at the knees, they should kneel onto the mat with the knees approximately

600mm from the end of the mat, before leaning forward and lying down flat with both hands under the chin. The head and shoulders should be raised until they are about 300mm off the ground with the hands still under the chin as though watching TV while lying on the floor.

Keeping the head still, the left arm should be extended and the left elbow moved forward about 300mm and placed on the mat with the hand turned so that it is palm upwards. The shooter should then position their left hand in order that they can hold the target between their thumb and forefinger. Keeping the left hand still, the shooter then moves the right arm and places it such that they are holding an imaginary rifle with their index finger extended to squeeze the trigger. This provides a basic position and the instructor will now be able to introduce the rifle, making minor adjustments to the positioning of the arms and hands as appropriate.

With the rifle held by the shooter, the instructor should position the handstop about 25mm in front of the left hand. Having correctly located the handstop, it is important for the shooter to take a rest as they may already be feeling uncomfortable from holding the rifle.

The sling can now be fixed to the jacket around the left arm and adjusted so that, when the left arm is extended, the clip/hook at the end of the sling does not quite reach the wrist.

Once rested the shooter lies back down on the mat and the instructor will clip the rifle onto the sling and assist the shooter to mount the rifle.

Once the rifle has been set up to fit the shooter, the shooter must then be able to get into position with the rifle and adopt the prone position. The following steps describe how to get into prone position with a jacket and sling:

■ Stand off the end of the mat facing the rifle.
■ Step forward and kneel down before lying down next to the rifle. Place the left elbow on the grip section of the mat.

■ Pick up the rifle with the right hand, keeping it pointing down the range towards the target at all times.
■ Hook the sling into the clip on the handstop using the left hand.
■ Place the left elbow near the front left edge of the mat.
■ Place the left hand above the sling but below the stock. The sling should be fixed to the upper arm and should wrap underneath the back of the left hand.
■ Raise the butt of the rifle into the right shoulder.
■ Adjust the body so that the rifle is level and move the left hand and elbow forward until the sling is taut. The hand underneath the rifle should be just touching the handstop and not pressed up against it too hard. The angle of the left arm should be equal on either side of the elbow and the left hand adjusted under the stock until it is comfortable.
■ Place the right hand on the pistol grip and keep the index finger on the stock. Do not put the finger on the trigger while getting into position.
■ Extend the right elbow to the right of the body until it feels comfortable. For high positions it will be close to the body, for low positions it will be further away.
■ Lower the head so the cheek rests against the cheek piece of the rifle and the eye is looking through the centre of the rear sight.

TEST AND ADJUST

Building a correct prone position takes time. Throughout their shooting careers a shooter will continue to change their position as their ability develops and as their body changes with time. The greatest amount of change takes place at the start, when the person shooting is getting used to the kit. There are so many possible positions for the body to lie

Sequence of shots showing the end to end process of getting into the prone position.

Connecting the sling 1. Pick up the rifle with one hand and hold the sling hook/clip in the other.

Connecting the sling 2. While holding the rifle, hook (or clip) the sling onto the handstop.

Connecting the sling 3. Keeping the rifle pointing down the range, raise the butt into the shoulder.

Connecting the sling 4. With the butt in the shoulder adjust the body position until the sling is taut.

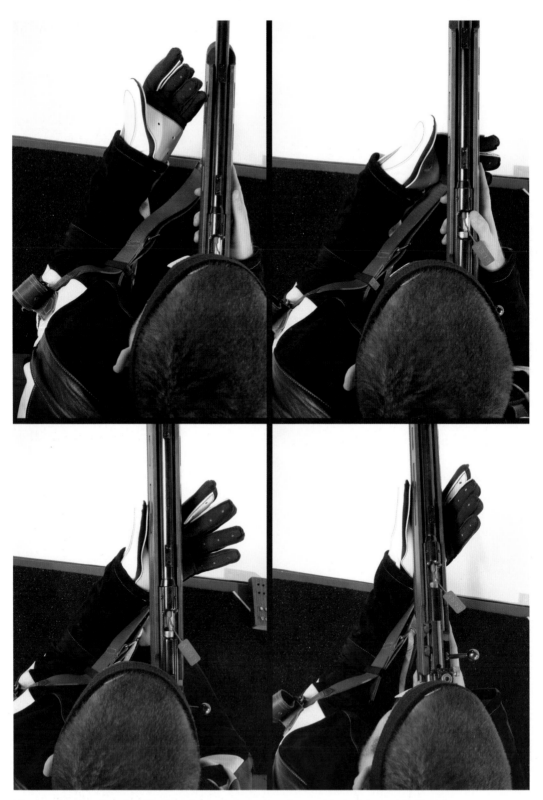

The hand supporting the rifle is positioned above the sling and below the stock. The sling must not be between the hand and the rifle, and it should be taut when correctly set up.

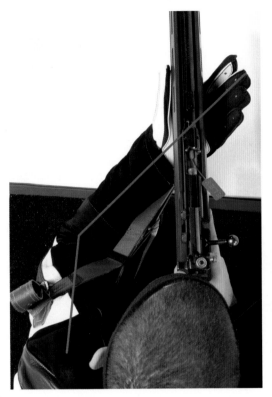

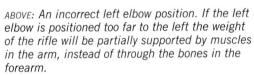

ABOVE: *An incorrect left elbow position. If the left elbow is positioned too far to the left the weight of the rifle will be partially supported by muscles in the arm, instead of through the bones in the forearm.*

TOP RIGHT: *Another incorrect left elbow position. If the elbow is too far to the right the body will not have lateral stability and will roll to the left, causing strain in the left shoulder and upper arm muscles.*

RIGHT: *In the correct elbow position the wrist, elbow and shoulder on the arm supporting the rifle should form a straight line.*

in, each minutely different from the other, that someone will never get into the perfect position first time. For this reason the shooter should try different positions to find out what works best for them.

Thinking about the position of the body, the shooter should only change one aspect of their position at a time and note the effect it has on comfort and stability. Each time something is changed the following question should be asked: 'Does it feel better or worse than before?' If it feels better – great; if it feels worse then the shooter should try a different position or move back to the previous position. The 'better or worse' question should relate to the comfort and stability of the position and not whether it makes the rifle point at the target.

It is important to remember that it is rare to change a single part of a position without also adjusting other elements of the position. If the left elbow is moved then the left hand may also need to move to keep the same angles each side of the elbow. This would in turn require the hand-stop to be moved and maybe the sling tightened or loosened. Each change will have a knock-on effect and so the shooter should not make one change, feel it doesn't work and change back without first investigating the possibility of the knock-on effects of the initial change.

Adjusting the Angle of the Left Arm

When getting down onto the mat the body will naturally be supported on the left elbow and the

To support the weight of the body when first getting into position the upper left arm is nearly vertical. This angle is not good for a stable or comfortable prone position.

The body has been moved backwards (away from the target) while keeping the left elbow in the same position on the mat. This movement should be done until the angle of the upper arm mirrors the angle of the forearm.

upper arm will be almost vertical. The shooter should keep the left elbow still and move the body backwards to change the angle of the upper arm so that it matches the angle of the forearm in relation to the ground.

Placing the Rifle Butt into the Shoulder

The butt of the rifle is a curved shape with a fixed or an adjustable butt plate made from either metal or plastic. This should fit firmly, but not too hard, into the shoulder. If the rifle is placed too high then the bottom of the butt will dig into the shoulder. Similarly, if the rifle is placed too low the top of the butt will dig into the shoulder. The padding in the jacket can make it difficult to tell exactly where the rifle

butt is located and the instructor should be able to help demonstrate the correct location. Depending on the rifle being used, it may be possible to adjust the butt provide a better fit to the shooter.

Left Hand Position under the Rifle

The left hand and arm support most of the weight of the rifle and it is important that they are both comfortable. The rifle position on the palm of the hand and the position of the hand in relation to the wrist can both have a great effect on the comfort of the shooter. A good hand and wrist position is comfortable and stable without relying on muscles to maintain the position. Once the shooter is in

LEFT: If the rifle is positioned too high in the shoulder, the head will be raised and the neck muscles will be strained.

RIGHT: With the rifle butt correctly placed in the shoulder, the neck will be relaxed and the eye can easily be positioned behind the rear sight.

LEFT: The rifle butt is positioned too low in the shoulder, forcing the head to angle forwards. This makes aiming difficult and can be uncomfortable for the shooter.

position, the rifle, hand and wrist can all be adjusted until they are comfortable. A common mistake is to assume the first position obtained is the best one. This is only likely for very experienced shooters and at this early stage time should be taken to ensure the position is comfortable.

COMMON ISSUES EXPERIENCED WITH THE PRONE POSITION

The following list includes the common issues experienced with a new prone position along with some of the ways these issues can be

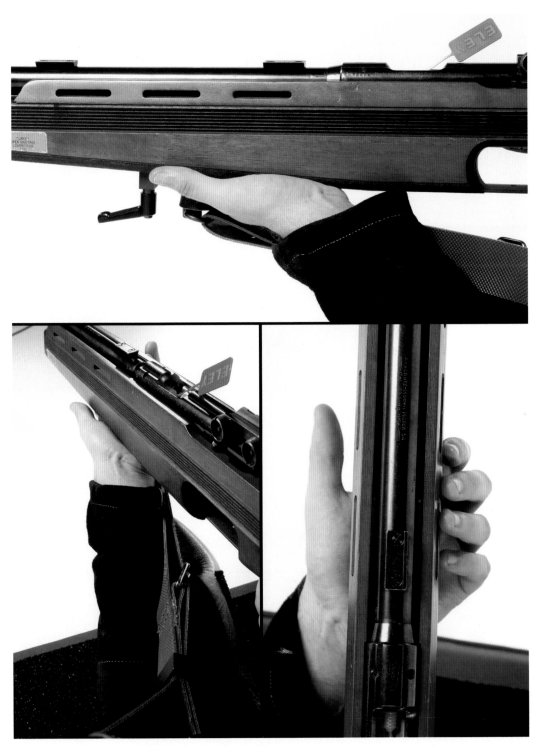

A good left hand position (shown here without a glove to aid clarity) has the rifle resting across the palm of the hand without any bends in the wrist, either vertically or horizontally.

resolved. It is important to note that there can be multiple causes for each issue and determining the cause requires a combination of experience and communication between the instructor and the shooter. The instructor can visually appraise the position, however, the way the shooter feels in their body (discomfort, strains, relaxed or tense muscles) can only be communicated with a good question and answer dialogue.

A bad left hand position. The wrist is straight but the rifle is resting on the thumb. This positioning can create pressure on the artery and reduce circulation, leading to pins and needles or general discomfort.

Another bad left hand position. The hand is twisted under the rifle, causing strain in the wrist, and the rifle is supported on the fingers. The weight of the rifle is held by the tendons in the wrist instead of being directed through the bones in the forearm.

Handy Tip

When you first start it is very difficult to know if your position is correct. Working with a partner can be helpful because, while one person is lying down, the other can look at their position and comment on what appears to be right or wrong.

- Sling is not taut: tighten the sling.
- Rifle feels like it is slipping down and to the right: either the sling is not tight enough or the left elbow is positioned too far to the left and needs to be moved to the right, creating a straight line between the shoulder, elbow and hand.
- Rifle feels heavy: the rifle weight is not fully supported by the sling and arm position. Tighten the sling and/or adjust the left elbow further forward and/or to the right.
- Pain in left wrist: usually caused if the wrist is bent and the muscles are being used to support the rifle on the left hand. This can be fixed by adjusting the location of the hand under the rifle to create a more natural position. Discomfort can also be caused by the sling being too tight; in this case lengthen the sling.
- Pain in left hand: hand may be pressing too hard against the handstop or the hand may be at an odd angle under the rifle. Adjust the position of the hand to relieve pressure or move the handstop forward and lengthen the sling.
- The head cannot get into a position for the eye to see through the sights: check if the rifle is the right size and if the sights are too far forward or back on the rifle. The shooter may be lying too straight in relation to the target and should increase the angle they are laying at. Alternatively, the butt

may be too high or low in the shoulder; check the butt is in the correct location in the shoulder.
- Pain in lower back or side: body is twisted or the torso is lifted too high off the ground. Check the body is laying straight and is not bent or curved; the left shoulder, hip and knee should be in a straight line. If the body is straight and the discomfort is not resolved a lower shooting position should be adopted (for descriptions of the high and low positions *see* pp.56–59).

The position might feel unnatural but it should never feel uncomfortable. If any discomfort is experienced the position is not right and something needs to be adjusted.

SHOOTING FOR THE FIRST TIME WITH A JACKET AND SLING

Building a Comfortable, Repeatable Position

When the shooter has found a position that is comfortable and stable it is good practice to unhook from the rifle and get up, before then getting back into position. During this process the shooter should be thinking about how they feel and whether the position feels the same as the previous one. Is it more or less comfortable? Has anything changed and if so then what is different? Once a comfortable, repeatable position has been built and the shooter is happy they are getting into the same position each time they lay down, the next stage is to try some live shooting.

Loading

To load the rifle the shooter's hand moves from the pistol grip to pick up a live round, insert it into the breech and close the bolt (or Martini action lever). This movement will require the right elbow to be raised off the mat and can cause the body position to shift. Sometimes this movement can be quite substantial. Throughout this operation the rifle must always remain pointing down the range towards the target.

The shooter must always be aware of the direction the rifle is pointing. If the rifle moves in a 'wild' or erratic manner then the shooter is not completely in control of the rifle and this is a safety issue.

Group Sizes

A shooter who is progressing from shooting with a rifle on a stand to shooting with the rifle using a jacket and sling will usually experience a large and visible change in the apparent quality of their shooting. The group size is likely to become larger and this can be perceived as a backward step that some people find disheartening. There is no need to worry about this change as it is perfectly normal. As the prone position is improved and corrected the group size will get smaller.

SHOOTING WITH A JACKET AND SLING: DOS AND DON'TS

- Do make sure the rifle, jacket and sling fit correctly.
- Do make sure the position is comfortable.
- Do check the hand supporting the rifle is between the stock and the sling.
- Do test and adjust: the first position adopted is not always the best position.
- Do concentrate on all of the core skills: they all work together to make a good shot.
- Don't put up with pain or discomfort.
- Don't forget to keep the rifle pointing down the range at all times.
- Don't be satisfied with something that is not right: take time to get it right and the shooting will be more comfortable and more accurate.
- Don't worry about group sizes, they might get bigger when the stand is removed but they will improve over time.

CHAPTER 6

IMPROVING THE PRONE POSITION

The first challenge faced by shooters who have progressed to using a jacket and sling is, as described in Chapter Five, how to get into a comfortable and repeatable prone position. Achieving a comfortable and stable position is an important part of consistent shooting, but equally important is that the position is aligned properly with the target.

If the shooter has achieved a comfortable prone position but they are not aligned with the target, muscle tension must not be used to move the rifle to the correct aim. In Chapter Four it was shown how easy it is to miss the centre of the target. A movement of only 0.25mm is enough to miss the centre by 6mm at 25 yards. Holding this level of accuracy with muscles is a very difficult task.

This chapter introduces the concept of natural alignment. A method known as 'test and adjust' can be used to help achieve the alignment more easily.

NATURAL ALIGNMENT

Natural alignment is the direction in which the rifle is aiming when the shooter is in the prone position and their body is completely relaxed. This is simple to describe but difficult to achieve in practice. When looking through the sights the natural instinct is to note where the rifle is pointing and then, using the muscles in the arms and shoulders, adjust the aim so that it points at the centre of the target. This use of muscles can be almost subconscious and is one of the leading causes of poor group size for shooters once they have started to shoot using a jacket and sling. It has the additional side effect of making the arms tired after a prolonged period of shooting.

For a position to be truly naturally aligned, the body must support the rifle so that it points at the centre of the target without any muscular effort.

The following exercise will demonstrate the impact of body position on the natural aim of the rifle and should only be done *before* loading the rifle:

- Set up a firing point and a target.
- Get into a comfortable prone position with an empty rifle.
- Aim at the target as though about to fire a shot.
- Close eyes and take a couple of breaths.
- Open eyes and do not move the rifle.
- Notice where the rifle is aiming in relation to the target: the aim, for example, could be high and right or a little low but in the middle (referring to the left/right alignment).

If the rifle is not aiming at the centre of the target after the eyes were closed then the prone position is not naturally aligned. To achieve a natural alignment the alignment of the body should be adjusted, tested (as described above) and adjusted again if necessary until the rifle naturally points at the centre of the target.

ADJUSTING BODY POSITION

As has been mentioned many times already, it takes only a tiny movement in the rifle position to make a very large change in the position that the bullet strikes the target.

Adjusting the alignment of the body is usually achieved by moving the hips and rotating the body position around the left elbow, which should remain stationary. The reason for keeping the left elbow in the same position is that it provides a pivot point for adjusting the aim up or down, as well as left or right, while also providing a point of reference to gauge how much adjustment has been made.

Pivoting the body around the left elbow moves the sight picture in the opposite direction to the direction the body moves. For example, if the natural alignment of the body is aiming to the left of the target, the shooter should move their body to the left, which will move the rifle aiming line to the right. Likewise, if the natural aim is too low, the body should be moved backwards. This has the effect of pivoting the front of the rifle upwards and thus raising the aim upwards too.

The legs should always be moved in the same direction as the hips by enough distance to keep the position correct. When the movement has finished the shooter should have the same shape of position but be pointing in a new direction.

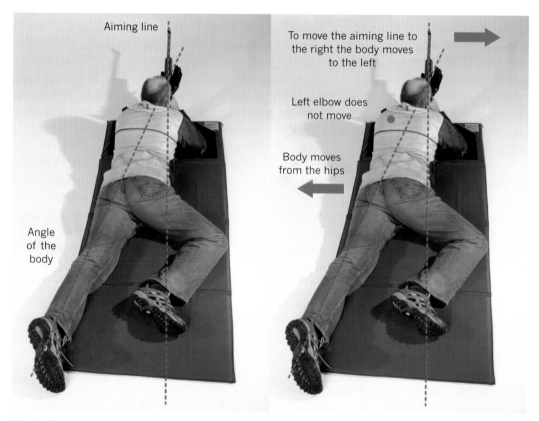

To change the aiming line to the left or right, the shooter must move their entire body, pivoting around the left elbow.

As the body moves forwards, the rifle, head and shoulders rotate around the left elbow and the aiming line angle moves down

The body moves forwards

Original aiming line

The muzzle moves down

New aiming line

To adjust the aiming line up or down, the shooter moves forwards or backwards, pivoting around the left elbow, which remains in the same position on the mat.

Using Test and Adjust to Correct Natural Alignment

Format: Shoot a five-shot group on a single diagram.

Core focus: Using test and adjust to correct the body's natural alignment.

Description: This exercise demonstrates how the body uses muscles to compensate for a lack of natural alignment. It also shows how a very small movement in the shooter's position can cause a very large change in the sight picture.

Method

1. Get into the prone position with the rifle pointing at the target.
2. Aim at the target as though about to fire a shot.
3. Close eyes and take a couple of breaths.
4. Open eyes and do not move the rifle.
5. Notice where the rifle is aiming in relation to the target: the aim, for example, could be high and right or a little low but in the middle (referring to the left/right alignment).
6. Without adjusting the body close the eyes again.
7. With the eyes still closed, adjust the position of the body by moving the hips and legs, in the direction and by the amount that should bring the aim onto the centre of the target.
8. Get comfortable, take two breaths and open the eyes.
9. Notice where the rifle is aiming.
10. Repeat the previous steps until the rifle is pointing at the target each time the eyes

are opened again and then shoot the five-shot group.
11. After the five shots repeat steps 3, 4 and 5. See if the position has changed during the five shots.

Usual result: The first position a person lies in is not usually the correct one: the first time the eyes are opened it is very unlikely the shooter will be aiming at the centre of the target.

Adjustments in the body need to be much smaller than most people think. The first time the shooter adjusts the body with their eyes closed they are most likely to overshoot the centre of the target and will be aiming in the opposite direction from their first attempt.

Checking the natural alignment at the end of the exercise will show if the position is stable and consistent, and if it has changed during the course of the exercise.

Additional focus: Throughout the exercise the shooter should think about how a very small movement in the body can make a very large difference in the direction of aiming.

Over time it will become more obvious to the shooter how much the body should be moved to adjust the aim. Experience will enable them to make small adjustments in order to bring the natural alignment onto the target. During the early stages of learning a shooter could spend a very long time adjusting their position and not firing any shots. A balance must be found between adjusting position and practising shooting. Remember that shooting live rounds also practises the other skills, such as breathing, aiming and trigger control.

After opening their eyes after an 'eyes closed' test, a shooter can see the natural alignment is wrong and causing the rifle to aim high and left, and should close their eyes and adjust their position (the aim should be on the top left spot on the target).

After adjusting their position based on an 'eyes closed' test, new shooters often adjust too much and find they are aiming in the opposite direction to their first position (the aim should be on the top left spot on the target).

CHAPTER 7

IMPROVING GROUP SIZE AND CONSISTENCY

The previous chapters describe in some detail how a new shooter can get into the prone position while remaining consistently comfortable and stable. This chapter provides information on topics that may not immediately come to mind, as well as a number of exercises that can help to develop the skills of breathing, aiming, trigger control, follow through and natural alignment. The exercises will help a shooter progress to the point where they can take the next step and shoot a scored card.

It can be rewarding to be able to put a value on ability and provide something that can be used as a mark of progress and improvement. Many sports have some measure of standard, such as coloured belts to mark the grade in martial arts. In shooting, the skill of an individual can be seen by the scores they achieve. However, many shooters progress to shooting 'scored cards' before they are truly ready and this can prevent them from progressing, as their goal becomes getting a better score instead

Improving consistency should result in a smaller group size.

of improving the skills to maintain a smaller group size.

Unless the shooter has developed their core skills to be able to shoot a group where most of the shots are inside the 9 ring on the target, they will only achieve slow progress when shooting scored cards.

SETTING UP THE FIRING POINT

Setting up the firing point is a simple way to help improve consistency and yet its importance is often overlooked. Simple things like the position of the mat and the location of the ammunition in relation to the shooter will make a difference to the comfort of the shooter and the ease of simple actions such as loading.

Mat Position

The shooting mat should be placed at an angle to the firing line. The angle of the mat will vary in relation to the angle at which the shooter lies and at a subconscious level can affect the angle at which the shooter will lie. The mat should be placed to match the position of the shooter and not the other way around.

If the shooter lies at an angle of 20 degrees to the target, then the mat should be placed at an equal angle. If the mat is aligned straight on to the target (perpendicular to the firing line) then the shooter may subconsciously lie down straight on to the target and this will not help a naturally aligned position to be developed.

In competition the space available to a shooter will be a 1m wide section of the firing point that extends back from the firing line

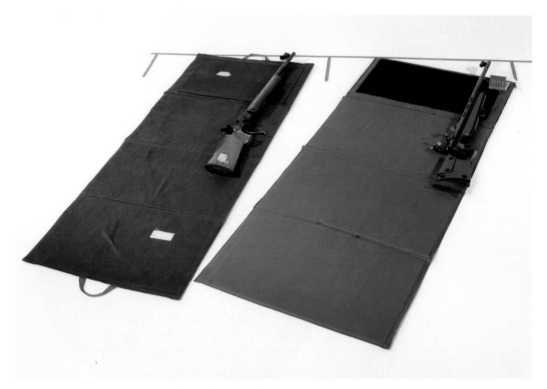

People shoot at different angles but must always remain within the 1m firing point limit. Here the mat on the right is at too wide an angle and spreads across two firing points.

ABOVE: A left-handed shooter positioned on the right allows plenty of space for both competitors.

BELOW: Left- and right-handed shooters should be careful not to place their mats too close together, otherwise their positions might interfere with each other.

By moving their mats further apart (but still within the 1m lane width) the shooters do not get in each other's way.

(away from the target). All of the shooter's equipment, and limbs, must remain inside the area while shooting and cannot spill over into the lane on either side. This may not sound like much but is sufficient for most people. At higher levels of competition the use of firing point space is strictly enforced. If the shooter lies at a wide angle they may find their extended leg encroaches on the next firing position. The rules for this are much more relaxed outside competition, but consideration for fellow shooters should be maintained. It is the responsibility of each individual to be aware of how their position may affect other shooters using the range.

If a left-handed shooter and a right-handed shooter are using firing points next to each other, it is advisable for the left-handed shooter to use the lane on the right-hand side as this reduces the likelihood of their feet getting in the way of the other. If the mats are positioned correctly, however, it is possible for a left-handed shooter to be on the left.

Ammunition Position

If the placement of ammunition on the mat is not considered when setting up the firing point, the shooter may find they have to move their body a long way to reach the ammunition

ABOVE: To reach a badly positioned ammunition block, a shooter may have to move their arm and sometimes their body a long way. This can disrupt the natural alignment of a position.

BELOW: With the ammunition block in an easily reachable position, the shooter only moves their arm a small distance and the prone position is not disrupted.

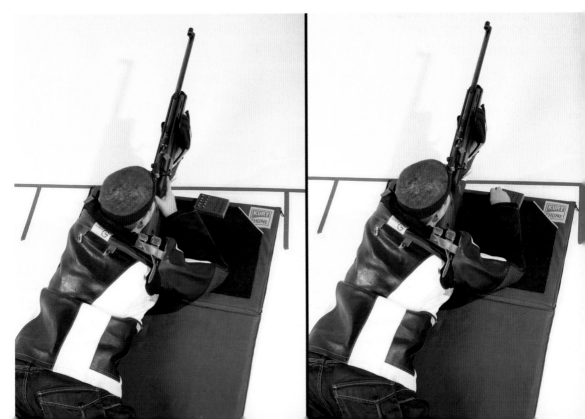

between each shot. Large movements will alter the alignment of the body, as well as causing the rifle to point away from the target and perhaps even cause discomfort to the shooter.

It is easier to load if the ammunition is placed within easy reach. This is usually somewhere on the mat near the front right edge, but this will vary depending on the shooter's position on the mat. Having to stretch to pick up a new round can cause the rifle to move and point in an unsafe direction, and it can also change the position of the shooter, affecting the consistency of their shooting.

Scope Position

Up until now there has not been a requirement for a scope to be used, although new shooters may have noticed others using a scope to view the target between shots. The use of a scope, as well as its benefits and drawbacks, are discussed in Chapter Nine, but at this stage a shooter will not benefit from having a scope.

EXERCISES TO IMPROVE GROUP SIZE AND CONSISTENCY

The following exercises are based on the information covered up to this point and cover the topics of breathing, aiming, trigger control and position. They can be performed at any time by persons of any level of ability. They do not need to be done in order, although for novice level shooters it may be beneficial to follow the order given here because some exercises rely on knowledge and skill gained in a previous exercise.

For each exercise a few lines are provided on the most likely outcome to help the shooter interpret their results. However, if the group sizes being shot are quite large it may not be possible to see some of the differences described.

1. Smooth Trigger Control

Format: Shoot two five-shot groups on different diagrams on a single target.

Core focus: The motion used to squeeze the trigger.

Background and description: Shooters may find they have shot a group with most of the shots falling in roughly the same location but that some shots appear away from the main group. There are many reasons this can happen: a common one depends on how the trigger is used while shooting. A smooth trigger action that is consistent should be used for each shot.

This exercise will demonstrate the difference in group size when the trigger is not used smoothly.

Method

The first five-shot group should be taken following these steps:

1. Adopt the prone position as usual, then test and adjust the position until comfortable.
2. Load, breathe and aim as usual.
3. When the sight picture is correct the trigger should be squeezed fast and hard.
4. Fire the five-shot group with a fast and hard trigger action.

The shooter should move to the second diagram and prepare to shoot the second five-shot group using the following method:

1. Test and adjust the position until comfortable and the position is naturally aligned with the target.
2. Load, breathe and aim as usual.
3. When the sight picture is correct the trigger should be squeezed smoothly, taking up the first stage of the trigger (if there are two stages). Pause when the second stage is reached, check the sight picture and then

squeeze the trigger through the second stage and firing the shot.

4. Hold the trigger for a further count of two and then gently release it.
5. Fire the five-shot group with a smooth and consistent trigger action.

Usual result: The first five-shot group is usually larger, and positioned lower and further right on the target than the second group. The second group is less likely to have shots that appear a long way from the main group.

Additional focus: Throughout the exercise the shooter should continue to focus on maintaining a good, naturally aligned position and a consistent, clear sight picture for each shot.

2. Natural Alignment

Format: Shoot two five-shot groups on different diagrams on a single target.

Core focus: Natural body position aligned with the target.

Description: This exercise is designed to show the importance of having a natural alignment with the target when in the prone position. If the position does not provide a relaxed alignment with the centre of the target the shooter must use muscles to force the rifle onto the target. This introduces movement in the position and will increase the group size.

Method

Shoot a five-shot group on a target using the position and alignment the shooter feels is correct.

Shoot a second five-shot group on a different diagram following these steps:

1. Get into the prone position with the rifle pointing at the target.
2. Close eyes.
3. Test and adjust the position until comfortable while keeping the eyes closed.
4. Open eyes and do not move the rifle.
5. Notice where the rifle is aiming in relation to the target.
6. Without adjusting the body, close eyes again.
7. With the eyes still closed, adjust the body in the direction and by the amount that should bring the aim onto the centre of the target.
8. Get comfortable and open eyes.
9. Notice where the rifle is aiming.
10. Repeat steps 4–9 until rifle naturally aims at the target and tracks vertically through the target when breathing.
11. Shoot the five-shot group.

Usual result: In most cases the second shot group will be a better (smaller) group than the first. If the shooter spends a long time adjusting for each shot in the second group, however, they may become tired and the group size can increase.

Additional focus: Throughout this exercise the shooter should also maintain their focus on a smooth trigger action, steady breathing and a clear sight picture.

3. Breathing

Format: Shoot a five-shot group on a single diagram.

Core focus: Maintaining a consistent breathing pattern for each shot fired.

Description: This exercise helps a shooter practise a steady breathing pattern for each shot fired. It also indicates if the breath is held for too long: a breath should never be held for longer than 4 or 5 seconds when taking a shot.

Method

Shoot a five-shot group on a single diagram following these steps:

1. Get into the prone position with the rifle pointing at the target.
2. Test and adjust the position until comfortable.
3. When the position is correctly aligned the shooter should load and prepare to fire the shot.
4. Breathing should remain steady and natural while the sight picture is aligned.
5. When the sights appear aligned, take one or two slightly deeper breaths (not full deep breaths, but just slightly deeper than the natural breaths taken previously).
6. After the deeper breaths the shooter should exhale until the sight picture is properly aligned. The target should appear to lower into the centre of the foresight.
7. When the sight picture is correctly aligned, hold the breath (lungs half full).
8. Check the sight picture is correct. This stage should take no more than a few seconds. If more than 4 seconds is taken the shooter should start to breath again and move the focus of the eye away from the sights without moving the head. Then go back to step 4 and repeat the process.
9. Fire the shot.
10. Exhale and take another couple of slightly deeper breaths to replenish the oxygen in the blood.
11. Repeat the process from step 4 to step 10 for each of the four remaining shots.

Usual result: The shot group may appear to be a little larger than usual. This is because the shooter is focusing on the breathing at the expense of other skills areas, such as sight picture or prone position alignment. The exercise is used to highlight that breathing is an important part of the process for firing each shot but should not be focused on at the expense of other skill areas.

Additional focus: Throughout this exercise the shooter should also maintain their focus on the alignment and comfort of the position, a smooth trigger action and a clear sight picture.

4. Sight Picture 1

Format: Shoot two five-shot groups on different diagrams on a single target.

Core focus: Focusing on the foresight instead of the target.

Description: This exercise repeats one given earlier in Chapter Four. It demonstrates the importance of focusing on the foresight rather than on the target.

Method

Shoot a five-shot group on a single diagram following these steps:

1. Adopt the prone position as per usual and test and adjust the position until comfortable.
2. When the position is correctly aligned, the shooter should load and prepare to fire the shot.
3. When aiming the eye should focus on the foresight element and the target should appear as a slightly blurry spot in the centre of the foresight element.
4. Shoot each of the five shots with the eye's focus being solely on the foresight.

Shoot the second five-shot group on a fresh diagram following these steps:

5. Adopt the prone position as usual. Test and adjust the position until comfortable.
6. When the position is correctly aligned the shooter should load and prepare to fire the shot.
7. When aiming the eye should focus on the target and the foresight element should appear as a slightly blurry circle around the clear spot that is the target.

8.   Shoot each of the five shots with the eye focus being solely on the target.

Usual result: Although the two groups may appear in different locations on the target, the first group should be smaller than the second. The eye will naturally align a blurry spot inside the centre of the foresight, but it is more difficult to place a blurry circle accurately around a clear spot.

Additional focus: Throughout this exercise the shooter should also maintain their focus on their natural alignment with the target, the comfort of the position, free and controlled breathing and a smooth trigger action.

5. Sight Picture 2

Format: Shoot two five-shot groups on two diagrams.

Core focus: Positioning the foresight in the centre of the rear sight.

Description: This exercise helps practise positioning the foresight in the centre of the rear sight. Often a new shooter will have the target in the centre of the foresight but not have the rear sight correctly aligned. A core reason for this is the difficulty in clearly defining the edges of the rear sight.

Method
Shoot the first five-shot group as usual, doing what feels right and using the technique that feels best.

Shoot the second five-shot group on a fresh diagram following these steps:

1.   Adopt the prone position as usual. Test and adjust the position until comfortable.
2.   When the position is correctly aligned the shooter should load and prepare to fire the shot.
3.   When aiming the focus should be on the foresight element. The target should appear as a slightly blurry spot in the centre of the foresight element.
4.   Check the amount of 'light' visible either side of the foresight. If the light is even on the left and right the sights are aligned centrally in the horizontal plane.
5.   Check the amount of light visible on the sides and top of the foresight. If the amount of light on the left, right and top of the foresight is the same it is centrally aligned in both the vertical and horizontal planes.
6.   Holding this position, check the target is aligned in the centre of the foresight. If the target is not in the centre the body's natural alignment is not correct and should be corrected.
7.   If the sight picture is aligned, fire the shot. If the prone position requires adjustment repeat step 3 through to step 6.
8.   Fire all five shots using this method.

Usual result: The first group should be larger than the second. The second group may be in a different position on the target, but do not worry about this. The size of the group is the key measure in this exercise, not the proximity to the centre of the target.

Additional focus: Throughout this exercise the shooter should also maintain their focus on their natural alignment with the target, the comfort of the position, free and controlled breathing, a smooth trigger action and a clear sight picture.

6. Putting It All Together

Format: Shoot two five-shot groups on two diagrams.

Core focus: Everything that has been learned up to now.

Description: This exercise brings together everything learnt by the shooter into a single exercise that highlights the importance of focus on every key skill for each shot fired.

Handy Tip

Do not stare at the sights. Ensure the eye is relaxed, otherwise the image will become distorted and the eye may begin to water.

Do not aim for too long. An expression sometimes used is 'acquire but do not admire': once the sight picture looks right take the shot. If the shooter focuses for too long on the sight picture it will become unsteady. The focus should be for no longer than the length of time the breath is held (4 or 5 seconds).

Method

For the first five shots the shooter should do exactly what they feel is right. Each shot should be fired using the technique with which they feel comfortable.

The second five-shot group should be shot by focusing on everything that has been learned. Concentrating on every step for each shot may seem like a lot to think about, but the checklist is used by top-level shooters for every shot they fire:

1. Get into the prone position with the rifle pointing at the target.
2. Close eyes.
3. Test and adjust the position until comfortable while keeping the eyes closed.
4. Open eyes and do not move the rifle.
5. Notice where the rifle is aiming in relation to the target.
6. Without adjusting the body, close eyes again.
7. Adjust the body in the direction and by the amount that should bring the aim onto the centre of the target.

8. Get comfortable and open eyes.
9. Notice where the rifle is aiming.
10. Repeat steps 4–9 until the rifle naturally aims at the target and tracks vertically across the target when breathing.
11. Breathing should remain steady and natural while the sight picture is aligned.
12. When the sights appear aligned take one or two slightly deeper breaths (not full deep breaths but just slightly deeper than the natural breaths taken).
13. After the deeper breaths the shooter should exhale until the sight picture is properly aligned. The target should appear to lower into the centre of the foresight.
14. Check the amount of 'light' visible either side of the foresight. If the light is even on the left and right the sight is aligned centrally in the horizontal plane.
15. Check the amount of light visible on the sides and top of the foresight. If the amount of light is the same on the left, right and top of the foresight, it is centrally aligned in both the vertical and horizontal planes.
16. Holding this position, check the target is aligned in the centre of the foresight. If the target is not in the centre, the body's natural alignment is not correct and should be corrected.
17. When the sight picture is correctly aligned, hold the breath (lungs half full).
18. Check the sight picture is correct. This stage should take no more than a few seconds. If more than 4 seconds is taken the shooter should start to breath again and move the focus of the eye away from the sights without moving the head. Then go back to step 4 and repeat the process.
19. When the sight picture is correct and the breath is held, squeeze the trigger smoothly, taking up the first stage of the trigger (if there are two stages), pausing

when the second stage is reached. Check the sight picture and then squeeze the trigger through the second stage firing the shot.

20.   Hold the trigger for a further count of two and then gently release it.

Usual result: This exercise can have two outcomes:

Result 1: The second group (total focus) will be noticeably better than the first group, because every single step for each shot has been thought through and executed in a smooth and natural way.

Result 2: The second group (total focus) will be noticeably worse than the first group: this is because some people focus on thinking about each step rather than actually applying them. If the prone position is not set up correctly this too will cause the group to be worse, because the shooter will remain in position for an extended period and any deficiencies in the position will begin to affect the shooter as either tiredness or discomfort.

Whichever outcome is achieved the exercise is a good one to demonstrate just how many things there are to think about when taking each shot.

A regular outcome of this exercise is that the shooter becomes aware that they occasionally miss a step out when taking a shot. Taking time to think through the shoot after it has been done will help to highlight anything that was difficult, forgotten or inconsistent – as well as highlighting what went well and felt good.

Additional focus: None – everything should be focused on in this exercise.

EXERCISE

Prone rifle shooting is often, and incorrectly, seen as a physically easy sport. Lying on the ground while occasionally moving the head or hands cannot possibly be physically demanding, can it? It is easy to see how some might think this doesn't require any physical fitness.

It is true that the sport does not involve the same exertions as experienced when playing rugby or swimming, but athletes in shooting events must maintain a precise control over every muscle in their body for extended periods of time and this requires a high level of fitness. To be able to maintain a solid and stable prone position during an event requires endurance, suppleness and a very precise physical control over the muscles in the body.

Physical training has other benefits, such as improved concentration and a reduction in levels of stress and nerves. World-class shooters spend as much time tuning their bodies physically as they do on technical training. Exercise and physical training should be a core part of every shooter's weekly routine. In addition, shooters should warm up and stretch before they shoot – every time.

It is not the intention of this book to provide detailed physical training plans or descriptions of exercises. Instead the reader should seek guidance from a professional fitness instructor at a local gym or leisure centre.

STRETCHING AND WARMING UP

At the start of the Olympics or any other high-level event, shooters can be seen warming up and stretching behind the firing point. Footballers, boxers, gymnasts, swimmers – in fact generally all sports people – warm up and stretch before competing. Yet in the UK it is very rare to see anyone at club level preparing in this way before they shoot.

Stretching loosens up the joints and can release tension in the muscles and tendons. For a shooter who wants to be relaxed on the firing point, stretching makes a lot of sense. Relaxing the arms and shoulders, neck and back will all help the shooter settle into a more comfortable and relaxed prone position.

Increasing the heart rate a lot before shooting may not be a good idea, but warming up does not need to raise the heart rate very much to still be beneficial. A slightly elevated heart rate can increase the flow of blood to and from the lungs and also increases alertness, both of which are very helpful for shooting.

It is important to note that if the reader has any medical condition or concern they are encouraged to seek medical advice before undertaking any warming-up programmes or exercising.

IMPROVING CONSISTENCY: DOS AND DON'TS

- Do take time to set up the firing point correctly. The precise placing of the mat is important to help build a naturally aligned prone position.
- Do keep the shooting mat within the 1m width of the firing lane.
- Do consider others using the range. Be aware of anything that encroaches onto someone else's firing point.
- Don't put the ammunition too far away, otherwise it will be difficult to reach.
- Don't worry if the results seen after the exercises differ from the 'usual result described'. This information is for guidance only and may not be true for everyone.

CHAPTER 8

USING THE SIGHTS

All the practice exercises given so far have focused on group size rather than how close to the centre of the target the group appears. Shooters may find that while practising different techniques their groups have appeared in different locations on the target. Such variations can happen without making any adjustments to the sights because there are many factors that can influence the group position, such as natural alignment, sight picture, trigger control and the position of the head and eye behind the rear sight.

Once a consistent group position is achieved, the sights can be adjusted to bring the group into the centre of the target. The sights on almost all small-bore rifles are adjustable. Usually the rear sight can be moved up, down, left or right in relation to the rifle. On some rifles the foresight can be raised or lowered. Moving the sights has the effect of moving the central aiming line of the rifle and changes the position of the group on the target.

When the foresight and rear sight are correctly aligned, the rifle is pointing in a specific direction. When the sights are adjusted the position of the rifle must also move to keep

A set of basic sights.

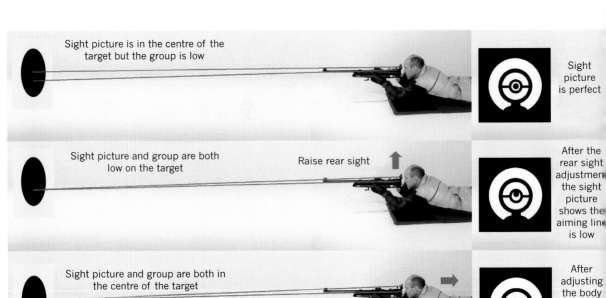

Sight picture is in the centre of the target but the group is low

Sight picture is perfect

Sight picture and group are both low on the target

Raise rear sight

After the rear sight adjustment the sight picture shows the aiming line is low

Sight picture and group are both in the centre of the target

Adjusting the body backwards raised the aiming line

After adjusting the body the sight picture is once again perfect

Sight adjustments are needed if the group is not in the centre of the target when the sight picture is correct.

the sight picture correct. This means the rifle will be pointing in a slightly different direction.

ADJUSTING THE SIGHTS

Most rifle rear sights are adjustable in two directions; vertically (elevation) and horizontally (windage). Changes can be made independently so the sights can be moved up without moving either left or right, which allows for a greater accuracy of adjustment.

Adjustments are made by turning the dials on the top and side of the rear sight, either clockwise or anticlockwise.

Adjusting Elevation

Turn the top dial anticlockwise to move a group up.

Turn the top dial clockwise to move a group down.

Adjusting Windage

Turn the side dial anticlockwise to move a group right.

Turn the side dial clockwise to move a group left.

The dials do not turn freely, but move in a series of movements known as 'clicks'. Each click corresponds to a single adjustment in the sight position, with the distance the sight moves determined by the type of sight and the number of clicks per 360 degree turn of the dial. There are usually ten or twenty clicks per turn on modern sights, but some older sights have eight or sixteen clicks to a full turn.

The distance a group moves on the target for a single click will depend on the type of sight and the range at which the shooter is firing. At 100 yards, using a sight with ten clicks per turn, a single click will move the group 4mm on

ABOVE: Older rifle sights have adjustment dials on the top and sides for elevation and windage changes.

BELOW: A high-quality modern rear sight. The dials on the top and side of the sights turn to move the aperture in relation to the rifle's line of fire with greater accuracy than in older rear sight models.

The scales on the side of the rear sight show the vertical position of the sights and enable changes to be tracked and recorded. A similar scale is found on the top of the sights to measure windage.

the target: a sight with twenty clicks per turn will move the group 2mm in the same situation.

SHARING SIGHTS WITH OTHER CLUB MEMBERS

If rifles are being used by more than one person at a club, the sights might be adjusted differently by each person and it can be easy for a shooter to lose track of their correct sight position.

Each shooter should always make a note of the position of their sights when they finish shooting and check that they are in the same position when starting to shoot the next time. This not only prevents disappointment when the first group appears away from the centre of the

target, but also saves time trying to adjust the sights to bring the group back to the centre.

Sight position is usually shown on a scale on the top and side of the rear sight. The scale shows the position either side of the centre mark. Keeping a record of the scale position will enable the sights to be checked and set correctly every time the rifle is used.

CHASING ERRORS

When adjusting sights it is important to make sure the reason for the adjustment is genuine. If the group is always hitting the target low and right, even when the shooter tries different trigger techniques or a slightly altered body position, then adjusting the sights is probably a good idea. However, if the shooter usually hits the target in or around the middle, but on one occasion finds they are shooting far to the left, it is more likely to be body position that has changed, not the sights.

Sights should be adjusted to bring the centre of the group into the middle of the target. This should never be done after a single shot as this can result in the shooter chasing their own errors. Chasing errors will be covered again later when introducing the use of a scope (*see* Chapter Nine) .

USING A BLIND

The human eyes work as a pair, focusing together to be able to judge distances and reacting together to different light conditions. The pupil contracts in bright light to limit the amount of light getting into the eye and becomes larger in dark conditions to allow as much light as possible into the eye. Both pupils should always be the same size, otherwise the brain cannot create a clear image from the different light conditions in each eye.

If a shooter has both eyes open they will see two different views of the target, one through the sights and the other looking along the side of the rifle. These two images will be seen at the same time and most people find it difficult to focus on the sight picture.

A simple solution is to close the eye that is not looking through the sights, but this causes a different problem. If one eye is shut the pupil in that eye will want to expand because it is in the dark, but the other eye will want to have a smaller pupil because it is in the light. Because the pupils must be the same size, a compromise is made and neither eye has the pupil at the size it should. This results in the open eye having a pupil that is too large and lets in too much light.

The solution to both problems is to block the image seen by the eye that is not behind the

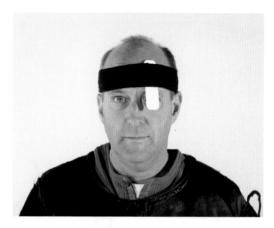

The blind is wide enough to block the image of the target but narrow enough to let light into the eye. It is held in place with a headband.

sights, but to still allow light to enter the eye, so keeping a balance between the light in both eyes. This is done using something held in front of, but not covering, the non-aiming eye. Such an item is called a 'blind' and usually comprises thin strips of card or plastic held in position with a headband. Commercial blinds can be purchased, but a home-made version made from card or translucent plastic, such as that used for plastic milk bottles, can do just as well.

USING SIGHTS: DOS AND DON'TS

- Do adjust the sights to bring the centre of a group into the centre of a target.
- Do use a blind when shooting and keep both eyes open.
- Don't adjust the sights after a single shot as this can result in chasing errors.
- Don't use a dark-coloured blind as this reduced the light that reaches the eye.
- Don't shoot with sights set up for another shooter (when sharing kit). Make sure the sights are adjusted according to the logs kept in your notebook.

CHAPTER 9

USING A SCOPE WHILE SHOOTING

The use of a scope (short for telescope) has not been covered in this book until now because it will not have benefited the shooter and may in fact have distracted the shooter from their practise. Scopes have both great advantages and equally great disadvantages. As with any piece of equipment there is a right and a wrong way to use one.

A scope enables the shooter to clearly see where their shots are hitting the target while remaining in position on the mat. Being able to see where the shots are hitting the target allows the shooter to make adjustments to their position or sights to ensure their group is in the centre of the target. Scopes are essential for competition shooting because they enable the shooter to see if they are hitting the target in the expected location.

The two separate items that are collectively known as the scope are the telescope and the stand used to support it. Scopes must provide, as a minimum, enough magnification to allow the shooter to see the hole in the target clearly at a distance of 15 or 25 yards; this requirement is extended to 50m or 100 yards if the shooter wishes to progress to outdoor shooting. The

Scopes are used in competitions and sometimes when training to see where shots are hitting the target.

magnification should be adjustable to allow the scope to focus on the target at different ranges. The stand should be sufficiently adjustable that the scope may be positioned at the correct height for the shooter and does not interfere with the ability of the shooter to lie in the correct prone position on the mat.

THE KIT

Activities such as bird watching and photo-graphy have produced a high demand for scopes and there are many different types available on the market. Some specially designed shooting scopes are available, but in recent years the trend has been towards using general-purpose scopes.

At a very basic level – and ignoring filters, different magnification options and price – scopes fall into two categories: the aligned eyepiece and the angled eyepiece. Deciding which scope to use is a personal choice and a

A high-end, plastic-bodied scope with a range of magnification adjustment options.

ABOVE: *The scope used here is an older model with a straight eyepiece. These are quite common in local clubs.*

LEFT: *Two scopes, one with an in-line eyepiece and another with an angled eyepiece. The latter has a padded cover to help protect it from damage.*

novice should try as many types as possible before deciding which is the best.

Scopes available to borrow at clubs are usually older models with basic magnification adjustment, although scopes are available with a range of magnification and filter options.

Straight Scopes

The less common, and usually older, style of scope has the eyepiece aligned along the main axis of the scope. The body of the scope must be positioned directly in front of the shooter so they can look through it.

Advantages: The scope can be placed directly in front of the non-aiming eye, so the shooter will not need to move their head very far, if at all, to be able to see the target through the scope. This lack of movement helps maintain a consistent body position and can help prevent group size increases through excessive movement.

Disadvantages: The position of the scope can get in the way when the shooter adjusts body position to move around a ten bull target.

It can be difficult to get the exact position of the scope right because the non-aiming eye has a blind in front of it and the scope must be in a position to look through without the shooter needing to move the blind.

Angled Scopes

The more common type of scope has an eyepiece set at an angle to the main axis of the scope. The body of the scope can be positioned to the side of the shooter instead of needing to be directly in front of the eye.

Advantages: The angle of the eyepiece allows the scope and the stand to be positioned further away from the shooter, so they are less likely to get in the way of the arm that supports the rifle. The scope can also be positioned to the side of the shooter, allowing the non-aiming eye to look around the edge of the blind and into the scope.

Disadvantages: The position of the scope and stand on the firing point can be greatly varied, unlike a straight scope, which must almost be directly in front of the shooter to be useful. This ability to vary the position can mean a shooter may not take as much care as they should when setting up the scope, and it is easier to put the scope in a bad position that requires a large movement of the body to get the eye to look through it.

Scope Stands

Whatever the type of scope used, it is advisable to support it with a proper shooting scope stand, not with a tripod. Shooting scope stands provide off-centre support, allowing the scope to be positioned close to the shooter's head without getting in the way of the arm that is supporting the rifle. The shape of the stand means it can be positioned at the front edge of a shooting mat with the legs still touching the solid surface of the ground instead of the soft, movable surface of the mat.

Tripod stands can be adjusted in height, but often the minimum height is not low enough for many shooting positions. This means the scope stand is dictating the height of the shooting position and may be forcing the shooter into a position that is not right for them, so making it harder to shoot either consistently or comfortably.

Specialist shooting stands are adjustable to almost any height required by a shooter. Some also have useful attachments for fine adjustment of scope direction and focus that can be used without moving out of the prone position.

ABOVE: The tripod stand for this scope is resting on the mat and one of the legs is touching the left arm of the shooter.

BELOW: A scope stand designed for shooting has legs that spread around the edges of the mat. This prevents the scope being dragged along unintentionally if the mat is moved and allows plenty of room for the left elbow to be positioned.

USING A SCOPE

Where to Place the Scope on the Mat

When setting up the firing point the scope should be placed at, but not on, the front left corner of the mat (or at the front right corner for left-handed shooters). The scope should always be placed on solid ground so that it will not be affected by the movement of either the shooter or the mat. If any part of the scope stand is on the mat the shooter can unknowingly move the position of the scope while adjusting their position. While this movement may not have a direct effect on the shot that is taken, it may indirectly affect the shooter's concentration, because changing the scope and realigning it may take their focus away from shooting.

The ideal position is to have the scope placed close enough to the shooter so they can see through it without moving their head very far, but far enough away so that it is not knocked by the shooter when adjusting position. If the shooter needs to move their body after each shot to see through the scope, it is too far away and needs to be repositioned so that only the head needs to move.

With the scope positioned too far away the shooter must move their whole torso to be able to see through it. This is disruptive to the naturally aligned prone position.

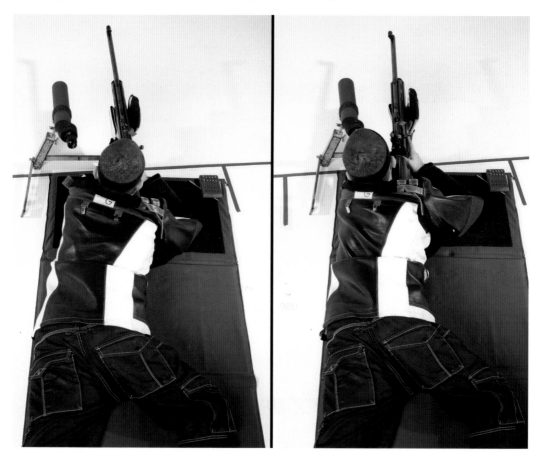

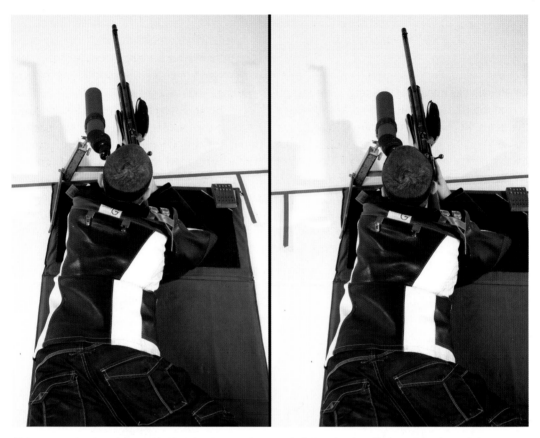

If the scope is placed correctly the shooter need move their head only a little to see through it.

It is easy to place a scope in any position near the mat and use it without thinking about its position in relation to where the body will lie. If a shooter usually lies on the right side of their mat, then the scope must be placed so they can see through it. Placing the scope far away on the left edge of the mat will require a large movement from the whole body in order to use it, which is very disruptive to a naturally aligned prone position.

Calling Shots

In general the scope should be used to confirm what the shooter already thinks. When a shot is fired the shooter should think about what they have just done and decide how they think the shot was. The two options are whether they think the shot was good, meaning it went close to the middle within the usual group size, or whether the shot was bad and went further away from the middle than was expected.

Being able to call shots is a skill in itself and will become easier with experience. The call will be based on knowing and feeling that everything about the shot was good or realizing that something was wrong with the execution, such as snatching the trigger or firing when the sight picture was not aligned properly.

Once the shot has been called the shooter can then look through the scope. What they see will either confirm their call or, if the call differs from the resulting shot, it will show that something else happened of which the shooter was not aware.

If a shot goes 'out', using the scope will never tell the shooter what went wrong but it should prompt them to evaluate what they did during the last shot and, once identified, fix it for the next shot. This 'fix' could mean adjusting the body position, taking more care on the sight picture or any of the other key areas to focus on while taking a shot.

Calling shots takes time to learn. Often a shot can be called high and right and the scope will show it is in the middle and far left. Making wrong calls can be confusing, but they will become less frequent as more experience is gained and ability increases.

Chasing Errors

When shooting and using a spotting scope the shooter is immediately aware if a shot did not hit the centre of the target. Even if the rifle is set up so the group is centred in the middle of the target, it can be tempting to adjust the position of the sights to bring some stray shots into the centre again. This temptation must be ignored. If five shots have been fired and they are all hitting the target in roughly the same place, with the centre of the group other than in the middle of the target, then the sights can be adjusted to bring the group into the centre of the target. This should, however, only be done if all other possibilities have been examined, such as natural alignment or trigger action.

An example of chasing errors and how it can result in bad scores.

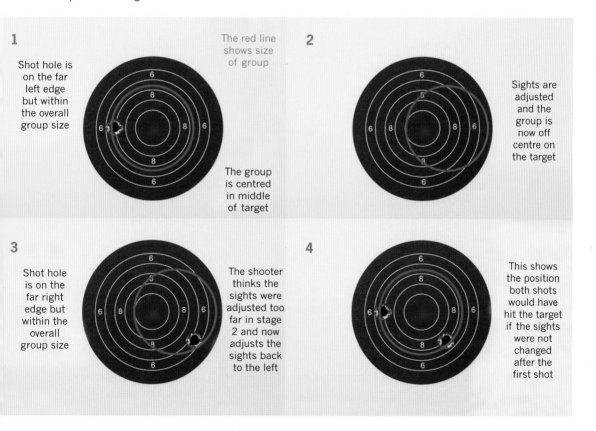

If the sights are adjusted after only a single shot has been fired then the shooter cannot be aware if the whole group is going to hit the target off-centre or if it was just a single bad shot. Adjusting the sights after a single shot is likely to make the next shot miss in the opposite direction: this is called 'chasing an error'.

PRACTISE EXERCISES

Using a Scope 1

Format: Shoot two ten bull targets on two different targets.
Core focus: Using the scope to see where shots have gone.
Description: This exercise introduces the use of the scope while shooting a ten bull scored card. The exercise should highlight some of the advantages and disadvantages of using a scope.

Method
Shoot a ten bull target following these steps:

1. Set up the firing point and place a scope at the front left edge of the mat.
2. Adopt the prone position and adjust both the scope and the body position so that the body position does not change when looking through the scope. The head can move but the movement should be as small as possible.
3. Shoot the first shot.
4. After the shot has been fired, look through the scope to see where the shot has gone.
5. Shoot the second shot.
6. Repeat steps 3–5 until the entire card has been shot.

Shoot the second ten bull target on a fresh target following these steps:

1. Remove the scope from the firing point.

2. Shoot the ten bull target as per normal.

When both targets have been shot the shooter should consider the following:

- When shooting with a scope, was the mind focused on each of the steps required for the perfect shot or was it thinking about how good, or bad, the previous shot was?
- When firing the last few shots, did the shooter know how many shots had gone 'in' and gained ten points?
- If a shot had gone badly and was a long way from the centre of the target, what happened on the next shot? What was the mind focusing on?
- Did knowing where a shot had hit the target prompt a change in body position or a sight adjustment between shots?
- Was the position of the scope sufficient that almost no movement was required to look through it after each shot, or was a large or awkward movement required?
- When shooting without a scope, how did it differ from shooting with a scope?
- Was the body position adjusted after each shot to a greater or lesser extent than when using a scope?
- Did the mind focus on the last shot fired or the shot about to be taken?

Usual result: The shooter may find their focus is on the shot that was just fired rather than the shot about to be fired. The loss of focus can be due to disappointment for a bad shot or over-confidence from a good shot.

A common mistake is when a shot misses the centre and the shooter then overcompensates for the initial error, causing the next shot to miss in the opposite direction.

It often happens that it takes longer to shoot targets while using a scope, since the shooter will adjust their position more often

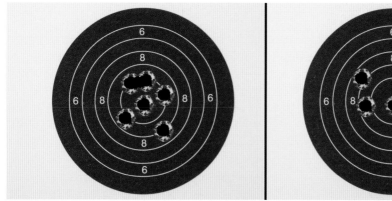

Both targets were shot by the same person. The one on the left was shot without using a scope. The one on the right was shot while using a scope to check each shot position. After finishing both targets the shooter stated that they felt under more pressure when using the scope, because they knew that the shots were not all good.

and spend time looking at the shots they have fired. If the cards are both scored, the non-scoped target often has a higher score that the scoped target.

Additional focus: Throughout this exercise the shooter should maintain their focus on natural alignment with the target, comfort of position, free and controlled breathing, sight picture and smooth trigger control.

The practise exercise using a scope can demonstrate the common issues experienced by new shooters. The scope provides an immediate visual result for each shot fired and this information can be very distracting. The scope by itself does not change the position of the shooter: it does not adjust the sights or alignment of the rifle and, if positioned correctly, should not interfere with the shooter in any physical way. What the scope does do is provide a mental distraction for the shooter and this can have a greater effect on someone's ability to shoot consistently than almost any other factor.

Using a Scope 2

Format: No shooting: setting up the position of mat, body and scope. An extra person will be required to move the scope for the shooter.

Core focus: Positioning the scope correctly on the firing point.

Description: This exercise does not involve firing any live rounds but instead practises setting up the firing point to suit the natural prone position of the shooter. This demonstrates the impact of incorrectly positioned scopes on the comfort and alignment of the prone position.

Method

Place a target at the end of the range so there is something to use for alignment and aiming, but do not fire any shots at it:

1. Set up the firing point without a scope.
2. Get into position on the mat, test and adjust as though about to start firing.
3. The second person places a scope so that the eyepiece is 15–30cm to the left of the non-aiming eye and a little in front of the shooter's head (this works for straight and angled scopes).
4. The shooter should align, aim and take a dry shot (firing the rifle without it being loaded), and then look through the scope. Pay attention to how far it is necessary to move from the prone position in order to see through the scope.

5. Try a couple more dry shots. The second person should then move the scope to a position where much less movement is required to see through it.
6. Take a few dry shots and consider how much movement is required to see through the scope in the new position.

Problems that may be encountered are that the stand does not fit around the edge of the mat, the scope stand knocks against the shooter's arm, or the scope can be distracting if it is too close to the non-aiming eye. Each situation should be overcome by changing the scope's position and/or the shooter's position in relation to the scope.

Usual result: The shooter will find there are some scope locations on the firing point that are better than others. The position of the scope in relation to the mat and the shooter will change for different types of scope and stand. Each time the firing point is set up the shooter should consider where the scope should be put to ensure that as little movement as possible is required to see through it.

SHOOTING SIGHTERS BEFORE STARTING A SCORED CARD

In theory a shooter should be able to lie down with their usual kit and hit the centre of the target with their first group of shots. For most people this is something that takes time and practice. Many find they need a few shots to help them settle into position. When shooting a scored card it is therefore a good idea for a shooter to check that they have set themselves up properly, are naturally aligned with the target, have a good sight picture and that the ammunition and scope are in good positions. This check should be carried out before firing any shots onto the main target.

The best way to check that everything is set up correctly is to fire some practice shots at a target that doesn't count toward the scored target. This provides an opportunity to correct anything that may not be quite right before the shooter moves on to the main scored target.

The non-scored target is often a spare diagram, or string of diagrams, placed next to the main target. These are known as sighters. Sighting cards can have as many or as few shots fired at them as the shooter feels is necessary (this may be limited by time in some competitions). Once the shooter is confident that the set-up is correct, they can move their aim on to the scored card. At any point the shooter can stop shooting the scored card and move back to shooting at the sighter if something needs to be corrected.

Sighters are shown on different sides of the targets. These can be changed according to shooter preference if the target boards can be changed.

CHAPTER 10

SCORED CARDS AND COMPETITIONS

SHOOTING A SCORED CARD

When a shooter is able to achieve a consistent group of shots in the centre of a target (inside the 8 ring) they are probably ready to shoot a scored card. Firing ten shots at a scored card is usually the first time a value or figure will have been put on the ability of a shooter. Up to this point the measure of ability has been the size and consistency of the shot groups. Although group size is a good measure of progress during the first stages of learning, it becomes less useful when the groups become smaller than 1cm across because it can be difficult to gauge improvement.

Shooting a target that can be scored provides an opportunity to track progress, although the score by itself is not a measure of success. Competitors at the top level tend not to focus on their scores but on the quality and consistency of their actions for each shot. At this early stage, however, score is a useful enough measure of ability.

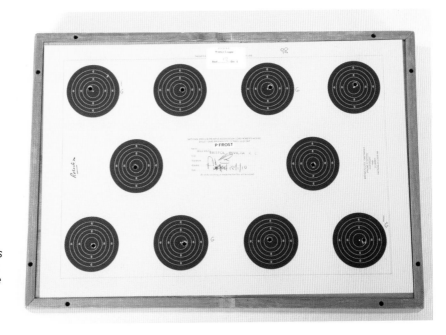

Scoring the shots on a target gives a shooter a score that becomes part of their average.

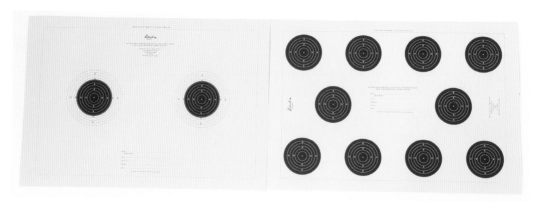

A two bull and a ten bull target: each target is named according to the number of diagrams (or spots).

Ten Bull Targets

It is possible to work out a score on any authorized target designed for small-bore shooting at a given range. The standard targets used for competitions, however, have ten diagrams and are known as 'ten bull' targets, where the term 'bull' comes from the term bullseye. A diagram is a black spot with scoring rings. The ten bull target has a single shot fired at each diagram with a maximum score of ten points being given for each shot. The maximum score for a single completed target is 100 points.

In theory, shooting ten single shots at ten diagrams should be no different from shooting a single group of ten shots at a single diagram. In both cases each shot is fired independently and the shooter is aiming for the centre of the target. In reality the ten bull target provides the shooter with some new challenges, many of which involve changing the body position for each shot.

Adjusting the Natural Alignment for Each Shot

When practising, the shooter usually takes time to set up in position, testing and adjusting until a natural alignment has been achieved. A minute or two may be spent settling into the correct alignment before taking the first shot. Each subsequent shot, however, takes less time because the position is already correct.

With a target that has ten separate diagrams the shooter's body position must be adjusted for each shot taken otherwise they will not be naturally aligned. A common mistake it to assume that, because the distance between each diagram is small, it will not matter if the aim is adjusted using the muscles in the arms instead of moving the whole body. Using muscles to adjust the aim might appear to work when moving between one or two diagrams, but depending on muscles to move around ten diagrams on the target will bring about a bad result. The shooter needs to spend time before each shot moving and adjusting their natural alignment onto the new diagram.

The result of not moving the body between each shot is that the shots will tend to appear not in the centre, but in the direction of the previous diagram shot. If the target is shot across the top from left to right, for example, then the first shot might be in the centre, the second might be just to the left of centre, and the third and fourth shots are further to the left

A shot target showing how, through not aligning the body position between each shot, the shots along the top row have progressively missed in the direction of the previous target.

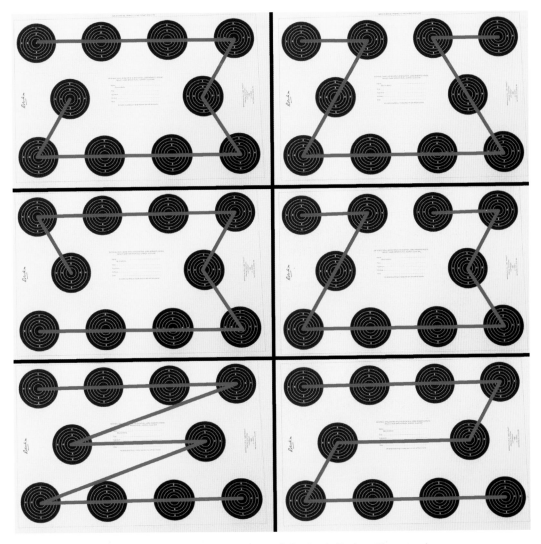

Various methods that may be used for moving around the card. Each pattern can be mirrored left to right.

because the natural alignment of the body is aiming at the first target on the far left. Sometimes this is so obvious that it is possible to guess the order that shots were fired by where they appear on the target.

There are many ways to shoot a ten bull target. Each of them requires ten shots to be fired and only one appearing on each diagram: the difference is in the order the diagrams are shot. There is no right or wrong way to move around the target but the accompanying diagram shows some of the more common methods, each of which is reversible.

Working Out the Score

There are two types of scoring: inward and outward. These terms define what happens to the score if a shot hole breaks a line on the target. Target diagrams have concentric circles, with each circle given a value. The centre circle

is worth ten points and the value of the circles decreases by a point per circle moving away from the centre.

A hole in the centre scores ten points. If a hole breaks a line and is in two target rings at the same time the score given will depend on the type of target being used: for an inward scoring target the higher score is given; for an outward scoring target the lower of the two possible scores is given.

Gauging Targets

If a shot hole is very close to a line on the target it may not be clear if the line has been broken. In these cases the shot hole must be gauged. There are many types of gauge available: some magnify the hole, while others penetrate the hole. Both make it possible to see if the shot has broken a line on the scored card. The most common gauge is usually made from brass and

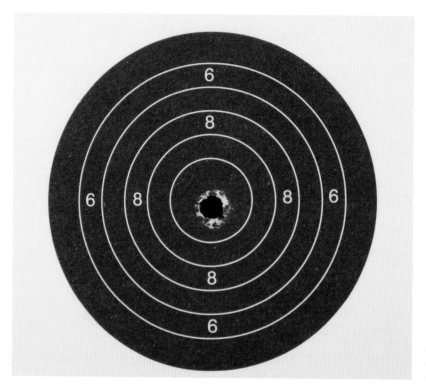

Ten points are given for a shot that goes through the middle of the target and does not break any lines.

A point is lost if the shot breaks the line between the 9 and the 10 ring on this outward scoring target.

looks a little like a child's spinning top. Different gauges are used for inward or outward scoring targets.

If using an outward scoring gauge the brass tip fits into the hole in the target and the wide body lies flat on the target surface. If the body of the gauge completely covers the next line out from the hole (away from the centre) then the shot has broken the line: for outward scoring this means the lower score is given. If, however, any part of the line remains intact then the shot is given the higher score.

It can sometimes be very difficult to tell if a shot is in or out. If the score for a practise card is being calculated, the gauge can be used whenever there is any doubt.

SHOOTING IN COMPETITIONS

There are many types of small-bore competition, each with a well-defined and detailed set of

A standard 22 outward gauge has a .22 diameter shaft that goes into the hole in the target and a flat disc that shows if the hole has broken the line. The disc also prevents the gauge from twisting and changing the size of the hole.

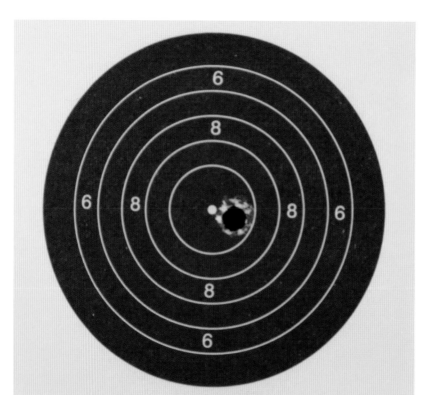

This shot appears to be in the 10 ring, but it is very close to the line and it is not clear if the hole has broken it.

With a gauge it is easy to see that the line is not broken and the shot scores a 10.

This shot also appears to be in the 10 ring, but the gauge shows the hole breaks the 10 ring and therefore scores 9.

rules and instructions. A comprehensive knowledge of the rules is not necessary for a person to be able to shoot in a competition but some idea of the basics will certainly help. The most likely starting place for competition shooting will be at a club as part of a team. Clubs can provide the support and guidance that help a shooter find their feet in competitions.

Most events are shot with the competitors divided into classes based on their ability (usually assessed from their average). A shooter can work out their average as either the average of all the scored cards they have shot or, more commonly, the best ten of the last twelve competition cards. The average for a person who has never shot in a competition should be taken from the last five to ten scored cards shot.

Whatever the type of competition, all that is required is that each shot hits the target in the middle. Sounds simple, doesn't it?

Types of Competition

This section provides general details about the types of competition available. There are too many variants to list them all and the finer details can vary depending on who organizes the competitions. This information is intended only as a guide and is not a definitive source: full rules and competition formats will be available from the event organizers.

Competitions can vary based on the distance from the targets, if they are held indoors or outdoors, the number of shots fired per target, the number of shots fired in total, team or individual participation, and what classes or divisions are available for entry. Matches may be shot and scored on the same day or the targets may be sent off by post to be scored by an official scorer and the results provided at a later date. Sometimes there may be a handicap scoring system.

Postal competitions. A team or an individual shoots a competition target that is usually marked by a sticker affixed to either the front or back of the target. The shot targets are then signed by the shooter and an independent witness before being posted to the official scorer. The results are returned by post or email at a later date.

There are both local and national postal competitions in which teams can shoot against clubs 5 miles down the road or 500 miles across the country. The benefit of a postal competition is that it can provide a greater variety of people and teams to shoot against compared to only shooting against teams within reasonable travelling distance. Postal competitions can also take the form of a knockout tournament or a league.

Shoulder to shoulder matches. Two or more teams, or individuals, shoot against each other on the same range at the same time while lying next to each other, quite literally 'shoulder to shoulder', on the firing point. The scores for the event are assessed when the shooting is finished and the winner is usually declared on the day.

Open matches. An extension of the shoulder to shoulder match, this is where a club, association, county or country hosts an event open to all shooters who meet the entry requirements. These events often have different classes to allow entrants at many levels of ability. The scores for the event are worked out after the shooting is finished and the winner is usually declared on the day.

National competitions. These can be run as either a postal or an open event, with competitors travelling to a single location. Sometimes the first few rounds can be arranged by post with the final being held as a shoulder to shoulder event.

Indoor competition. Usually shot at a distance of between 15 and 25 yards using standard ten diagram competition targets. Sometimes 50m events are held indoors; this is rare, however, because most 50m ranges are outdoors.

Outdoor competition. Usually 50m, 100 yards, or both, using standard competition targets. Competitions usually comprise one (or more) of the following event types:

- English match: 60 shots to count fired at 50m, with a total score out of 600.
- Scottish match: 60 shots to count fired at 100 yards, with a total score out of 600.
- Dewar: 20 shots to count fired at 50m and 20 shots to count fired at 100yds, with a total score out of 400.
- Double Dewar: 40 shots to count fired at 50m and 40 shots to count fired at 100 yards, with a total score out of 800.

When is a New Shooter Ready for Competition?

If the competition rules allow, anyone can enter, no matter what their level of ability, although they are expected to be able to handle the rifle safely and shoot without needing to have an instructor present. Even though it is theoretically possible to enter an open competition as an almost complete beginner, it is advisable for a shooter to be able to score 80 or above consistently on a standard ten diagram target before entering a competition.

Local clubs often have multiple teams, each comprising members of similar ability. This allows clubs to have teams of very good shooters and also of new shooters, both of which can enter competitions on behalf of the club. These teams can, and often do, compete in both local and national leagues. If the competition has different classes then a relatively new shooter can enter a lower class and should be shooting against people of a similar ability.

What is the Best Type of Competition to Start out with?

The best introduction to competition shooting for a relatively new shooter is to compete as part of a team for a local club. Shooting for a club team will provide the support of the other club members if the shooter is unsure of what they should be doing. Postal competitions are the usual starting point for club teams, later progressing naturally into shoulder to shoulder or local open events.

A barrier for new shooters entering open competitions will be their lack of personal kit. Open competitions usually require travel to a different club and it can be difficult to arrange the use of club kit and rifles away from the home range. The use of club kit away from the home range is something that is done at the discretion of each individual club and may not always be available. The use of club rifles away from the premises is restricted by the law governing ownership, transport and storage of firearms. Unless a person has their own Firearm Certificate they will be unable to take responsibility for a rifle.

Shooters wishing to compete in open competitions should take the next step and begin to purchase and use their own kit (*see* Chapter Fourteen).

Is Shooting a Competition Target Any Different from Shooting a Practise Target?

Assuming the type of target used for practise is the same as that for competition, there are technically no differences, as the same shooting techniques are required to hit the centre of the target for both categories. However, although there may be no technical differences between a practise and a competition target, there can be a psychological difference. A common term used in shooting is 'sticker-itis', an invented word (derived from the small stickers, attached to targets, that define the competition being shot) used to describe why a shooter does worse in competition than they do in practise. (Adding 'itis' to the word 'sticker' makes it seem like an ailment.)

People often have a different mental experience, and different scores, when shooting in a competition – whether it is a postal, shoulder to shoulder or an open event – to that which they have when practising. The difference, if not caused by external factors such as the weather, can be explained by the psychological effects of competing, worry about possibly losing or the chance of winning, the additional pressure of shooting within a set time limit or simply the fact that the competition is a visible public measure of a person's ability to shoot that can be seen by one's peers. Unfortunately there is no simple cure for these problems and each person must learn to deal with these pressures in their own way. Generally people find that over time the nerves will go away. As they become more accustomed to the format of competitions, and are more confident in their ability to shoot, the effects of 'sticker-itis' are greatly reduced.

CHAPTER 11

RIFLE CARE AND MAINTENANCE

Rifles are items of precision engineering that have finely adjusted moving parts (trigger and action) and very strong static parts that are put under great pressure each time a shot is fired (chamber and barrel). Rifles are designed to cope with regular use, but to ensure precision and accuracy for each shot they also require maintaining and this involves cleaning the rifle.

When using club kit it is important to follow the club rules and processes. Each club will have a policy about rifle care and cleaning.

Some clubs may insist on rifles being cleaned after every shooting session, whereas others might clean the rifles every six months. Whatever the club's policy, the basic methods used to clean the rifle are the same and are described here. More advanced tasks, such as cleaning the trigger mechanism, are mentioned but a detailed description is beyond the scope of this book.

Shooters are reminded that oils and cleaning agents are used when cleaning rifles.

Cleaning and maintenance is of great importance in looking after a rifle.

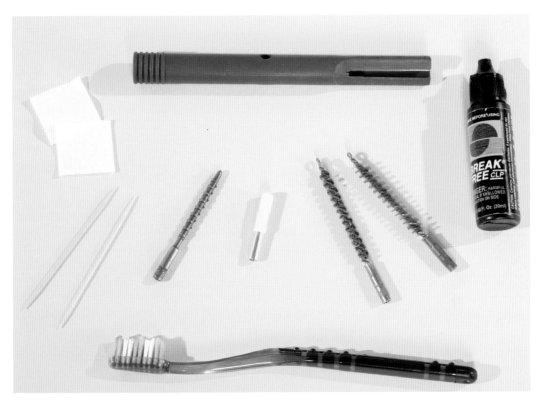

Cleaning equipment: cleaning rod, cloth patches, jag, breech guide, stiff brush, cleaning fluid and oil.

Appropriate protection should be used for the hands and eyes, based on the guidance given by the product manufacturer. Always wash your hands after cleaning any shooting equipment.

CLEANING KIT

There are some standard items that are used when cleaning a rifle:

Cleaning rod or pull through. This is used to push or pull cloth patches, or pellets, through the barrel.

Cloth patches. Special patches designed to fit in the barrel are used with a cleaning agent, with oil or dry. These are pushed or pulled through the barrel to remove dirt. Cotton pellets can be used instead of cloth patches if the cleaning rod and attachments allow.

Jag. A metal tool that 'grips' the cloth patch and fixes it to the end of the cleaning rod. If cloth pellets are used instead of patches a pellet holder will be used instead of the jag.

Breech guide. The guide fits into the breech of the rifle and prevents the cleaning rod from bending as it is pushed through the breech and into the barrel.

Stiff brush. Used to clean the breech and the bolt. Sometimes shooters will use an old toothbrush. The brush should be stiff but not abrasive: wire brushes should never be used.

Cleaning fluid. Small-bore rifles should be cleaned with petroleum-based cleaning agents because this helps to break up the dirt and residue inside the barrel and breech.

Oil. Gun oil is applied after cleaning to prevent water from forming as condensation inside the barrel.

Cocktail sticks provide a useful means of getting dirt out of cracks and tight corners in the breech or from the head of the bolt. Because they are made from wood or plastic, they are soft and will not damage or scratch the metal of the rifle.

HOW TO CLEAN THE RIFLE

Cleaning the Barrel and Breech

Every time a round is fired a residue of lead and accelerant is left behind in the barrel. This residue is pushed along the barrel by each shot and is forced under pressure between the side of the bullet and the barrel, causing the small particles to scratch the inside of the barrel. When the rifle is being used the residue is warm and pliable, causing little wear to the barrel. If the residue is left in the barrel at the end of the session, however, over a few days it cools and crystallizes into much harder particles. When the rifle is next fired these abrasive crystals are pushed down the barrel at great speed. Repeating this action many times is like sanding the inside of the barrel with a fine piece of glass paper and could lead to premature wearing of the barrel.

In addition, the barrel can get quite warm when in use. If it is not cleaned there is a risk that condensation will result when stored in the gun cupboard as the warm metal comes into contact with cold air. This condensation can cause small rust marks in the barrel, which will significantly reduce its life and may alter the barrel's performance.

The ammunition contains explosive and lubricant, a residue of which can be left behind in the chamber and breech when the round is fired. This residue builds up over time and can have a severe impact on the performance of the rifle, including stopping the bolt from moving and preventing the rifle from being unloaded.

Cleaning the Barrel of a Bolt Action Rifle

1. Remove the bolt from the rifle.
2. Remove the sights from the rifle to prevent them being knocked and damaged during cleaning.
3. Using a stiff brush (but not a wire brush), clean the breech, taking care to remove any build up from the corners of the breech and around the ejector pin (this is where the cocktail stick might be useful for the corners).
4. When the visible dirt has been removed, the breech should be wiped with a cloth patch coated in cleaning fluid. The cleaning fluid should be left in the breech for a few minutes to break up the remaining dirt. When ready, wipe down the breech with a clean patch or cloth.
5. When the breech is clean a breech guide should be fitted, sliding it into the rifle in the same way as a bolt. Different rifles require different methods to insert the bolt, so check the manual or ask for help if it is unclear how to insert the guide.
6. Fit the jag to the end of the cleaning rod and put a cloth patch, with a small amount of cleaning fluid, onto the jag. Make sure the end of the jag is completely covered by the patch so that the metal jag does not scratch the inside of the barrel. (If using cotton pellets, fit a pellet to the end of the rod.)
7. Push the rod through the barrel, starting at the breech, until it appears out from the muzzle. Remove the dirty cloth patch and the jag before pulling the rod back through the rifle. The jag is removed because it can scratch the inside of the

ABOVE: A toothpick can be useful for getting into tight corners when cleaning the breech.

BELOW: A breech guide is inserted in the same way as a bolt and prevents the cleaning rod from bending as it is pushed through the barrel.

A jag (with pellets) that has passed through the barrel. Note how the cloth pellet completely covers the end of the jag to prevent scratching the inside of the barrel.

barrel if it does not have a cloth patch around it.

8. Wipe the cleaning rod with a clean patch to remove any debris.
9. If the cloth patch was very dirty, another patch with cleaning fluid should be pushed through the barrel. This action should be repeated until the cloth comes out almost clean, remembering to wipe the cleaning rod each time before it is pushed through the barrel.
10. Fit a clean cloth patch to the jag and apply a small amount of light gun oil before pushing it through the barrel. This removes any excess cleaning fluid and leaves a thin film of oil to prevent any rust.
11. Push a dry patch or pellet through the barrel to remove any surplus oil. If this comes out clean the barrel is clean. It is important that any surplus oil is removed before using the rifle next time otherwise permanent damage can occur to the barrel.

Cleaning the Barrel of a Martini Action Rifle

The procedure to clean a Martini action rifle is similar to that of a bolt action rifle. The principal difference is that the falling block loading platform and trigger assembly must be removed from the action prior to cleaning. There is a single finger-tight bolt that passes through the action and trigger mechanism. Once this is removed the trigger mechanism may be extracted from the stock and the Martini action rifle can be cleaned in the same way as a bolt action rifle.

This bolt has not been cleaned and shows a build-up of waxy residue around the extractor pin. If not dealt with, this can cause problems when unloading.

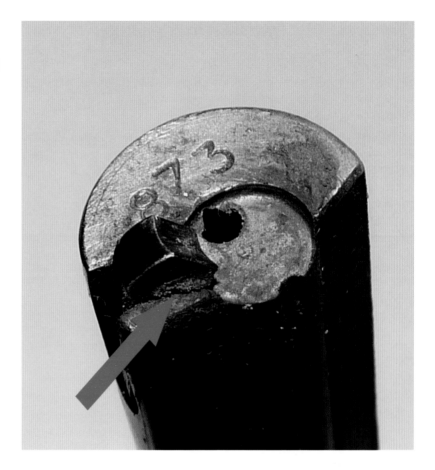

Cleaning the Bolt

The bolt is a critical part of the rifle and can become dirty very quickly. To fully clean a bolt it must be stripped down to its component parts. This is a complex task for someone unfamiliar with the kit and it is easy to lose the small springs that are inside the bolt, thus rendering the bolt useless.

At the beginner level, the bolt should not be fully stripped: a thorough external clean will prevent most problems from occurring. Some can shoot for years without cleaning their bolts and appear to have no problems, but this can be down to good luck. These simple steps can prevent a frustrating problem occurring unexpectedly.

The head of the bolt is the end from which the firing pin extends to strike the rim of the live round and also has either one or, more commonly, two extractor pins. The head of the bolt also forms the seal around the end of the chamber and withstands much of the force from the bullet as it is fired. Owing to the close proximity between the bolt and ammunition, the head of the bolt can become coated in the residue explosive and lubricant when a shot is fired in a similar way to the dirt build-up in the breech (*see* above). Residue on the head of the bolt can prevent it fitting snugly against the round when it is sealed in the chamber. The build-up can also prevent the extractor pins from moving freely: the most severe outcome of this is that the rifle will not unload without a large force being applied to the bolt.

To prevent excessive build-up the bolt should be cleaned regularly and the 'gunk' removed. A simple method, without damaging the head of the bolt, is to use a cocktail stick to remove any visible build-up from around the head and the extractor pins. The bolt can also be cleaned with cleaning fluid to help break up the dirt before wiping it with a cloth. If the extractor pins can move without sticking, and there is no visible build-up of residue, the basic clean is complete.

How Often to Clean the Rifle

There are many schools of thought on this subject, ranging from infrequently through to every time the rifle is used. For many shooters a rifle is a piece of precision-engineered equipment that should be cleaned and maintained after every time it is used. Other shooters may just put their rifle away after shooting and don't clean it for many years.

For a new shooter the most appropriate methodology is to clean the rifle after each time it is used. The sport is littered with numerous examples of the consequence of not cleaning a rifle, but it is extremely rare to hear about a problem arising from regular cleaning.

Finally, to prevent rust developing the external metal components should be wiped with a small amount of light oil before the rifle is stored, unless it is made from aluminium.

Dealing with a Stuck Bolt

One situation that can be caused by not cleaning a rifle is a stuck bolt. The rifle may fire, load and unload without any problems and then, without warning, the bolt can suddenly jam shut and the only way to open it is to apply a large force to the bolt handle. If this happens during a competition the shooter will probably have to forfeit the match because they will be unable to un-load the rifle. This can cause further disrup-tion because the rifle cannot be moved from the firing point with the breech closed and no safety flag visible. Usually the only thing to be done is for the shooter to leave the firing point and await the end of the detail, before returning to the rifle to try to open the bolt without distracting the other shooters. This is a rare occurrence but one that can definitely spoil a good shoot. Ensuring a clean rifle and bolt will help prevent things like this from occurring.

CHAPTER 12

AN INTRODUCTION TO OUTDOOR SHOOTING

The leading prone-position small-bore competitions, both in the United Kingdom and in the world, involve shooting at 50m and at 100 yards, with both distances being shot almost always outdoors. Shooting outdoors is very similar to shooting indoors. The need for a naturally aligned position, a consistent sight picture and all the other core skills is the same both indoors and out, but there are a few further topics that a shooter should know about before venturing outside.

When shooting outdoors the light conditions can vary from dark clouds to bright sunshine. There can be wind, rain or heat haze. All the

Outdoor shooting at 50m.

Some outdoor ranges such as this one, which is built in a quarry, have natural butts. Other ranges may use banks made from earth or sand to stop bullets behind the targets.

time the conditions can change between each shot the shooter takes. Learning about how the weather can affect each shot will help a shooter to improve their consistency and to understand why some of their shots might not have hit the centre of the target.

The format of competitions is different outdoors. Targets are also different, with more than a single shot being fired at each diagram. Scoring is calculated using inward gauging instead of the outward gauging used in most indoor competitions.

TYPES OF OUTDOOR EVENT

The standard 50m event is called an English match: this involves firing sixty shots and is scored out of 600. This is often followed by a 'final' with the top eight or ten shooters in the event firing an additional ten shots, which are scored to the nearest 0.1 instead of the nearest whole number; the maximum score for a shot is 10.9 for a 'dead centre' bull. This scoring method makes it easier to differentiate between the top shooters, who are sometimes separated by tenths of a point at the end of a match.

A similar event, known as a Scottish match, involves sixty shots fired at 100 yards. Unlike an English match, this event does not have a final. Shooting at 100 yards is often combined with shooting at 50m in events: Dewar and

Double Dewar matches involve firing twenty or forty shots at both 50m and 100 yards, with the total score from both distances being used to work out the winners.

When shooting indoors the weather will have almost no effect on how a person shoots, because they are generally protected from the elements inside a building. This all changes when shooting outdoors: varying wind and light conditions and heat haze can all have an effect on where a shot hits the target. Shooting in wind, through heat haze or dealing with changing light conditions are complex topics and are covered in Chapter Thirteen.

OUTDOOR RANGES

The layout of an outdoor range is very similar to that of an indoor range. They both include butts, targets, a range area, a firing point and a firing line. Sometimes the firing point is inside a building and the targets are outside. This means that the shooter is protected from the elements but still has to consider the effect of the weather while shooting. On other ranges the shooter can be outdoors without any cover at all.

Outdoor ranges have safety flags to warn people passing by that firing is in progress, as well as smaller wind flags to help the shooter

50m targets with backers. The numbers above the targets match the lane numbers to help the shooter know they are aiming at the correct target.

This 100 yard target has a single sighter positioned above two diagrams. Shots inside the black line all count toward the total score for the card.

gauge the wind (for more information *see* Chapter Thirteen).

SAFETY

The safety considerations while shooting outdoors are generally the same as when shooting indoors, with a few additional elements. Since there are no walls or ceilings to stop errant bullets, it is very important to keep the rifle pointing down range at all times.

Ear protection should be used when shooting and also if standing just behind the shooters at the firing point, since the sound is still at levels that can damage the hearing.

50M AND 100 YARD TARGETS AND BACKERS

The targets used at 50m and 100 yards are physically larger than those used at the standard indoor distances of between 15 and 25 yards, but they appear to be the same size when viewed through the sights because the targets are further away from the shooter. This means that the amount a shooter needs to move to miss the centre of the target and score an 8 at 20 yards is roughly the same as the distance they would move to score an 8 at 100 yards.

Targets at 50m usually have six diagrams: two sighters (the diagrams on the top row of the card) and four diagrams to score with five shots per diagram on the scored section. In some events, where Gehmann boxes are used, as few as two shots are fired per target. One reason for this is that, when scoring the cards for very good shooters, it is easier to tell how many shots there are on the target. If the shooter has put five shots in the same hole it can be difficult to tell if there are four or five shots, which can affect the scores. The whole target is scored out of 200.

Targets at 100 yards have three diagrams arranged above each other in a line. The top diagram is for sighting in and the lower two diagrams are scored. Each scored diagram should have ten shots fired at it and each diagram is scored separately, providing two scores out of 100 and giving a total score out of 200 for the whole target.

Backers

When shooting outdoors, targets will often come in two parts: the main target with the black scoring diagrams and a blank card the same size as the target. The blank card is positioned a short distance behind the target. This backer is important because it can resolve any disputes in the competition, such as cross shots. By overlaying the target onto the backer and lining up the holes from each shot it is possible to tell if a shot has come from either side of the shooter.

When a shooter has produced a very tight group it can be difficult to tell how many shots are in the group. If a target should have five shots on it and the group appears to have only four holes, the backer can be used to see if the additional round is in the group. This works because the additional distance between the backer and the target allows each bullet to continue on its trajectory once it has passed through the target and the groups appear slightly larger on the backer.

HANDY TIPS FOR OUTDOOR COMPETITIONS

Turning up at an outdoor event for the first time can be a little daunting. Although most shooters will attend events with people from their own clubs, here is some infoemation that may be of use. Events can be very different, but these general tips should help prevent any big surprises.

At outdoor events competitors are expected to change their own targets and time is allowed for this between details. For an English match at a level other than National or International there are usually three details of 20 minutes, with 10 minutes in between to change targets.

Each competitor is expected to take between twelve and sixteen large bulldog clips to an event, unless the targets are electronic or motorized target boxes. These are required to hold the target and backer to the target frames.

There are usually more competitors than there are firing points on a range. This means that during the 10-minute target change between details it is also necessary to either set up, or remove, all the kit from a firing point. At the end of their detail a shooter should clear their firing point quickly to allow the next person time to set up and prepare for their shoot.

Setting the Sights

Don't forget to adjust the rifle sights for the distance being shot. If the rifle has been used to shoot at 20 yards and is about to shoot at 50m, the rear sight must be raised to account for the additional distance. Depending on the type of sights used there is usually a fifteen 'click' raise required from 25 yards to 50 meters (30 clicks on more precise sights), and a fifty click rise from 20 yards to 100 yards.

It is always better to be safe than sorry, so if a shooter cannot remember if the sights have been adjusted they should change them anyway. It is better to hit the target too high than too low because the sighters are positioned above the scored targets. A low shot caused by not adjusting the sights can really spoil an otherwise good day.

CHAPTER 13

ALLOWING FOR WEATHER WHEN SHOOTING OUTDOORS

Moving from indoor to outdoor shooting provides new challenges to the small-bore rifle shooter and it also provides new excuses for missing. Excuses such as 'the wind pushed that one out' or 'the light was changing through that detail' can often be heard up and down the firing line, even if there is hardly a breath of wind at the time or only a small cloud passes in front of the sun. Understanding the weather and how it can affect a shot is an important skill and will help a shooter fire their shots at the best time in difficult conditions. Of course changeable weather and strong winds will have an effect on the sight picture and the trajectory of a bullet, but if a shooter can read the weather these effects are minimized.

UNDERSTANDING THE EFFECTS OF WIND

In flight, bullets are affected by three separate forces: gravity, air resistance and wind. Gravity pulls down on the bullet, air resistance (or 'drag') slows the bullet and wind moves the bullet sideways, up or down. Note the use of the word 'move' instead of 'push' in the previous sentence. The bullet is not pushed by the wind but its trajectory is changed by the effects of drag.

Another key element in how much a bullet is affected by the wind is the velocity of the bullet. The slower a bullet travels, and the longer it is in the air, the more it will be affected by the wind. This means the same wind direction and strength will have a greater effect when shooting at 100 yards than at 50m and this must be factored in when working out what adjustments to make for the wind.

Crosswind

A common misconception is that the wind pushes bullets in the direction it is blowing. The truth is that a crosswind turns the bullet slightly into the direction the wind is coming from and this creates more drag, slows the bullet down and makes it drift in the direction the wind is blowing towards.

Headwind and Tailwind

Headwinds or tailwinds have drag effects on a bullet, but to a lesser degree than crosswinds. A headwind will slightly increase the velocity of the bullet relative to the air it is passing though, which will increase the amount of drag. This makes the bullet both slow down and drop faster, so when shooting in a headwind the groups on the target will appear lower than expected.

A tailwind will reduce the drag and the bullet will not drop as quickly. The group will appear slightly higher than expected on the target.

It is very rare to have a direct head or tailwind

when shooting, as the wind will move around objects and the terrain will cause local fluctuations in wind direction. This means that whenever the wind is blowing there will be some element of crosswind for the shooter to deal with.

READING WIND DIRECTIONS AND STRENGTH

For shooters to be able to know the effect of the wind on a shot they must be able to identify and classify its strength and direction. There are many ways of reading the wind. The most commonly used methods have been around since the 1930s and possibly earlier. There are many data books and charts that can be used to work out the adjustments required when reading the wind, but this subject is not something that can be learnt solely from a book. It is a skill that will develop with practice and experience. One of the best ways to learn this skill is to listen to the other shooters at an event and try to use their experience along with the techniques given here to decide on the best way to tackle the wind conditions on the day.

Judging Wind Strength

Some ranges have high-tech anemometers (wind speed gauges), most will have flags at various positions on the range to indicate wind direction and strength, and others may have nothing at all to help judge the wind. As a general guide the following telltale signs can help a shooter work out the wind strength:

The most common visual aid at an outdoor event will be a number of wind flags positioned at various locations on the range itself. The stronger the wind, the higher the flag will raise. As a very rough guide the speed of the wind can be worked out by dividing the angle made between the flagpole and the centre line of the flag by the number four, which gives a rough speed in miles per hour. For example, a 60 degree angle between the flag and the pole shows a wind speed of 15mph. This is, of course, a very rough guide but it can still be helpful.

One of the best, but possibly the hardest, method for working out the wind speed is by watching the mirage. A mirage is usually seen on hot, sunny days but can also appear on overcast days in the right conditions. Mirage is recognizable by the wavy distortion when looking at an object in the distance and is caused by the reflection of light through layers of air that are at different temperatures.

If a shooter looks through their scope they should be able to adjust the focus so that the mirage is visible in front of the target. If there is any wind the mirage will appear to be moving in the direction the wind is blowing. In general a mirage can be used to gauge the wind accurately up to speeds of about 11 or 12mph. The only time a mirage is not helpful is when there is a direct head- or tailwind, in which case the mirage will appear to 'boil' and it is not possible to judge the strength of the wind.

Identifying Wind Direction

The best method is to use the clock system. The

0–3mph	Wind hardly felt, but smoke drifts
3–5mph	Wind felt lightly on the face
5–8mph	Leaves are kept in constant movement
8–12mph	Raises dust and loose paper
12–15mph	Causes small trees to sway

Wind flags help the shooter work out the direction and strength of the wind. Here there appears to be little or no wind and the flags are stationary.

Wind from 12 o'clock is a headwind and will cause shots to drop slightly.

Wind from 6 o'clock is a tailwind and will cause the shots to hit the target slightly high.

Wind from between 8 and 10 o'clock and from 2 to 4 o'clock is considered to be a full crosswind. This means the full effect of the wind will be felt by the bullet.

Winds from between 12–2, 4–6, 6–8 and 10–12 o'clock are considered to be 'half crosswinds'. This is because the wind is at an angle and the bullet will not be affected quite as much as it would by a full crosswind.

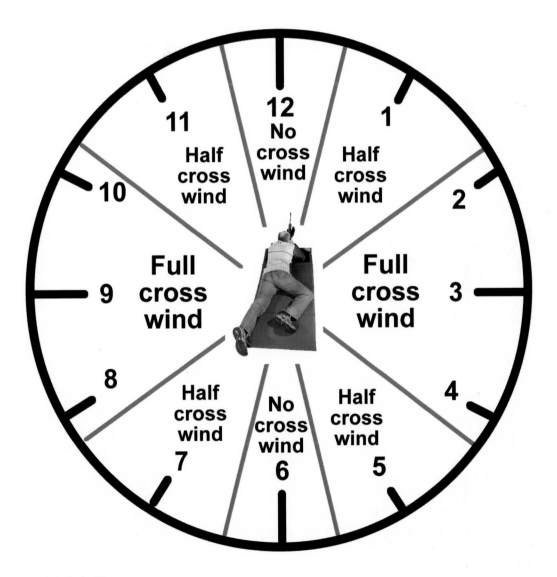

The 'wind clock'.

shooter should imagine themself lying at the centre of a clock face with the target at 12 o'clock. From this position the wind will be blowing from a direction that can be identified by the position of an hour on the clock face.

The value of the wind (full, half, tail- or headwind) combined with the strength of the wind will determine the amount of adjustment required by the shooter. Failure to notice and correct for a full crosswind will almost certainly result in a less than desirable outcome for a shot.

HOW TO SHOOT IN THE WIND

Shooting well in changeable wind conditions can be seen by some as a form of magic, by others as maths, while some people think it is down to luck. Whatever the belief of shooters in general, there will always be those who can shoot well in almost any conditions. These are the ones who are able to observe the conditions carefully and make the best adjustments to suit the circumstance.

There are two parts to shooting in the wind: one is to adjust the rifle sights correctly for the general wind conditions, and the other is to make sure that every shot is fired when the conditions are the same.

Adjusting the Sights in Steady Wind Conditions

Once the shooter has determined the wind direction and strength the next step is to adjust the rifle sights to compensate for the effect of the wind. If the rifle is already zeroed for the range, then the shooter only needs to make adjustment for the wind. If the rifle is not zeroed – perhaps the shooter has changed distance or not previously shot on the range – then sighting will naturally take into account the wind and when the group is centred the effect of wind will already have been accounted for.

To correct for wind a shooter can either make a series of sighting shots and adjust the sights based on what they see through the scope, or they can make an initial adjustment before firing a shot, to try to get the group roughly into the centre of the target, and then use their sighting shots to fine tune the position.

The amount to adjust will depend on the wind direction and strength as well as the degree to which the sights can be altered. If the wind is blowing left to right the shooter's group will appear on the target to the right of the centre. As a rough rule of thumb, a 2mph full crosswind from the left will move a shot from the dead centre of the target so that it breaks the 9/10 ring to the right of centre, and a 4mph full crosswind will move a shot to the 8/9 ring. As each type of rear sight can be different the amount of adjustment required can also vary. The shooter will become accustomed to their own kit and should know the number of 'clicks' required to move from the 8 ring to the centre, this should be the same number of clicks as for the equivalent adjustment indoors at a shorter range.

Once the group position on the target is centred, the shooter can move onto the competition card. As long as the wind remains constant most of the shots will fall inside the group size in the centre of the target. It is important to note that the wind is almost never constant and the shooter should keep alert for changes while they are shooting.

Shooting in Changeable Conditions

When preparing to take a shot the shooter must focus on all of their key skills (breathing, aiming and trigger control). In addition to these they must be aware of any changes in the wind. The conditions experienced at the start of a 20-minute shoot can be very different to those at the end, and in some cases the wind can change as often as every 10 seconds. If the

Wind conditions can be changeable, as can be seen by the varying positions of the wind flags in these photos, which were taken 10 seconds apart.

wind is changing strength or direction the shooter must ensure they are alert to these changes and only fire when the conditions are the same for each shot.

The way to do this is to keep an eye on the wind flags during the course of fire. If the flags change as a shot is about to be fired, then don't squeeze the trigger. If the wind changes there are two options available: either relax and wait for the wind to change back to the previous state or, if it looks like the wind has changed for more than just a brief moment, make the appropriate sight adjustment for the new wind condition. Never be afraid to go back to shooting on the sighter (if available) to check if the conditions are putting the shots in a new location on the target.

One technique that is used by more experienced shooters when the conditions are changeable or gusty is to centre the group on one side of the bull instead of in the very middle of the 10 ring. This has the effect of putting most of the shots just to the side of the centre, but if the wind changes slightly then the shot moves towards the centre instead of away from it. Of course, the effectiveness of this technique is determined by the ability to shoot a very small group and is not advisable for new shooters.

The simple rule is that if the wind changes, then do not take the shot. In a competition where there are time limits, however, it is not always possible to wait for consistent conditions and the shooter must make do as best they can. The thing to remember is that every competitor is dealing with the same conditions and so everyone is having the same issues. Although

This shooter is in the shade and shooting into bright sunlight. This can cause the sight picture to change and the eye to work hard while aiming. Under these conditions the shooter should rest their eye as often as possible.

reading the wind is important, it is the ability to apply the core skills properly for every shot that will have the greatest effect on a shooter's performance.

LIGHT CONDITIONS AND OTHER WEATHER EFFECTS

In addition to the effects of wind on the bullet, there are other weather conditions that can influence the outcome of a shot, such as the brightness of the light, shadows and mirage.

How Light Changes the Sight Picture

Light does not affect the trajectory of the bullet, but it does affect the way the shooter sees the target through the sights. The amount of light passing through the rear sight aperture changes the size of the pupil in the eye and this changes the apparent size of each element of the sight picture.

A minor effect of light conditions can be seen in the size of the target in relation to the foresight element. When the sun is bright the pupil is small and the target may appear larger in the foresight. Conversely, in dull conditions the target can appear to be smaller as the pupil size increases. This change can be seen as the target appears to fill more (or less) of the foresight element. Because it is difficult to change the size of the foresight element while shooting, most shooters will accept these changes. Some indeed may not even notice them, and instead the shooters concentrate on getting the correct rear sight size for the conditions.

Changing light conditions have a greater effect on the amount of work done by the eye to focus on the sight picture. When the sun is bright a lot of light will pass through the rear sight aperture and the ring of light around the target through the foresight will be very bright. This brightness makes it difficult to determine when the sight picture is properly aligned. Conversely, if the conditions are dull and not much light passes through the rear sight aperture, the target will then not appear well contrasted against the foresight and it can be equally difficult to determine the correct sight picture.

Each of these scenarios puts the shooter's eye under strain as it tries to focus. The way to reduce this strain is to use an iris on the rear sight of the rifle. An iris allows the size of the aperture to be increased or decreased to suit the light conditions. In bright sunlight the iris is used to decrease the aperture and the reverse is done in dull conditions.

Adjusting an iris is individual to each person as everyone has slightly different vision. If a shooter is using an iris they should experiment to find the best set-up for them in the conditions at the time. The optimal iris size is when the iris is reduced to the point just before the sight picture becomes darker. If the picture becomes darker then not enough light is passing through the iris and the eye will strain to see clearly.

Blocking Out the Sun

A more obvious effect of sunlight disrupting a shooter is when the sun is low in the sky and shines into the eyes. The sun does not need to be directly in front of the shooter for it to be

---

Bright Sunlight

Shooting in bright sunlight can be very tiring and can cause eye strain. Shooters should not focus for too long on a target in bright sunlight because this will burn a temporary image of the sight picture onto their retina. This is similar to the effect experienced after accidentally looking at a light bulb, when an image of the bulb is still visible even through closed eyes.

To prevent this happening the shooter should focus on the sight picture for only a few seconds and make sure they look away from the brightness between shots, so allowing the retina to clear the bright image.

---

distracting because rifles have shiny parts that can reflect light into the eye from unexpected angles.

Completely blocking the sun is bad because there will be plenty of light passing through the sights but none will be getting to the eye from around the sights. This causes the same eye strain as when one eye is closed (as described in Chapter Three). Instead, the direct sun should be blocked but enough ambient light allowed into the eye to prevent distortion of the sight picture. This is usually achieved with special hats fitted with side flaps to block out the sun.

HEAT HAZE

On warm days the ground heats the air above it and that air rises. This rising air forms layers of different air temperature and density. When light passes through these layers it becomes distorted and this causes objects to appear to shimmer. This is known as heat haze (or a mirage). For shooters this can be obvious when a mirage appears in front of the targets and the targets seem to shimmer in the distance.

Because the mirage is changing the path of light, the image of a target seen by the shooter is not in exactly the same position as the target. So when a shooter aims at the centre of the target as they see it, they are in fact aiming at an image of the target that is offset because of the mirage. On a day when there is mirage, shooters must adjust their sights to counter its effects. The amount of adjustment required will depend on the strength of the mirage and if there is any wind causing the distortion to move left or right.

Shooting Through Heat Haze

As when shooting in wind, shooters must keep an eye on the mirage: if it changes then so will the sight picture and appropriate changes to the sights must be made to keep the group in the centre of the target. Keep in mind that mirage also appears on warm days that are not necessarily sunny.

Adjusting the spotting scope so that it is focused on a position just in front of the target will show the heat haze clearly and this allows the shooter to observe it before making the necessary adjustments.

How much to adjust the sights will depend on the conditions on the day. Unfortunately this is not something that can be taught in a book. Each shooter must learn from their own experiences and use that knowledge each time they come across heat haze.

OTHER WEATHER-RELATED CONDITIONS

Rain, Sleet and Snow

Precipitation of any kind does not usually affect the trajectory of a bullet to any great degree. The usual result of rain is that the shooters get wet and targets can become soggy.

If going to shoot outdoors and it is raining, or is likely to rain, it is advisable to take some waterproof clothing and a cover of some kind to keep the ammunition dry. If there is thunder and lightening, shooters are advised to seek guidance from the range conducting officer as to whether it is safe for shooting to continue.

Mist and Fog

Mist and fog reduce visibility. Shooting in these conditions can be both difficult and dangerous: targets are not easily determined and the safety officer on the range may not be able to see if the range is clear. It is up to the range conducting officer to make a decision based on the conditions at the time and call off the events if visibility is too poor.

Events held in the spring and autumn can be affected by mist and fog if they start early in the morning. When shooting through a very slight mist, a shooter should remember that everyone is dealing with the same conditions and they should carry on as best they can.

Effects of Temperature

Temperature affects the shooter, ammunition and air density. Shooting in sunlight can be distracting if the shooter gets too hot and dehydration can affect the level of concentration. When ammunition sits in direct sunlight, the powder will burn at a faster rate, so changing the speed of the bullet. This in turn changes the position of the group on the target.

When sighting in under these conditions a shooter might expect to see a slight raise in position of their group on the target and should adjust their sights accordingly. It is unlikely that the temperature will change significantly while shooting, but the effect of sunlight on the ammunition can be significant, so keep the ammunition in the shade as much as possible.

CHAPTER 14

THE NEXT STEPS

This book has presented topics that will aid a new shooter in taking the first steps: from finding a club through to preparing for and shooting in outdoor competitions. The basic techniques for building a prone position have been described, along with core skills that should be leared if accurate, consistent shooting is to be achieved. This final chapter provides information on buying kit, owning a rifle and progressing to an intermediate level. These will most likely form the next steps in a shooting career, but no matter how far a shooter progresses, the core skills always remain the same and the early chapters of this book can be revisited at any time to brush up on the basics.

ACQUIRING PERSONAL KIT

When starting to learn to shoot, club kit is usually perfectly adequate, but eventually shooters will either want to use their own kit or they will be required by the club to allow other new starters to use the available kit.

Which items of kit to buy first and how much to spend will be up to the individual shooter. There is a healthy second-hand market for shooting kit as people often upgrade their own equipment or move away from the sport and no longer need it. It is usual to acquire kit over time, starting with the smaller items like slings, mats and ear defenders, before looking at the higher cost items such as scopes, jackets and

rifles. Some items of kit are quite generic (sling, scope) and some are personal: jackets and gloves must fit properly and be comfortable in order to be useful. These should be tried on to ensure a proper fit before purchase.

It is quite possible to pick up a jacket, sling, glove and mat for £200. Proper shooting scopes tend to cost a little more as they hold their value quite well, but should still be available for less than £100. The item that should always be purchased new is hearing protection, since the history and quality of second-hand ear defenders is difficult to determine.

Buying new kit instead of second-hand can be very satisfying and retailers offer a wide range of low and top brand kit. A new jacket can cost anywhere from £100 to £800 and it is possible to have one tailor made. There are pros and cons to getting a jacket made to measure: it will be a perfect fit and the colour and style desired by the shooter, but any change in body shape or size will turn a tailored jacket into a very loose or very tight-fitting jacket. Deciding to spend the money on a fitted jacket is a personal choice but new shooters are advised to try out various styles and look at second-hand jackets before spending any money.

OWNING A RIFLE

For many shooters the time will come when they want to own their own rifle. This might be

---

Choosing a Jacket

Shooting jackets are available in many different shapes and it is worth trying a few different styles before committing to buying one. It can be quite easy to like the look of a jacket and then find, after buying it, that it really doesn't fit very well.

When trying on a jacket, remember to lie down in the prone position with it on and done up. Wearing the jacket when standing up might indicate that the size is right, but it will not test the comfort when really needed in the prone position. Never feel ashamed of asking to borrow a mat so that the jacket fit and comfort can be tested in the prone position while still in the shop.

---

because club kit is now no longer available, the hassle of sharing kit becomes too much or simply owing to the desire to own a new rifle. Unlike the rest of the shooting kit, a rifle cannot be purchased without an official firearms licence and this involves a formal application process managed by the police.

Firearm ownership in the United Kingdom is controlled by extensive legislation with severe penalties for anyone who is caught operating outside the law. To preserve the integrity of rifle shooting as a sport, it is important for individuals to ensure they are aware of the law and keep up to date with changes as they happen. It is for this reason that a comprehensive description of applying for a firearms licence is not included in this book, but only a general overview of the basic process. Before applying, the reader should check with their local police firearms unit for the current requirements.

A person must be aged seventeen years or older to be granted a Firearm Certificate (FAC) in their own name. A firearm certificate may be granted to a person aged between fourteen and seventeen years of age (if they meet the required criteria), but they may not themselves purchase any guns or ammunition. No person under fourteen may be granted a firearm certificate, or use firearms other than on an approved range or shooting gallery.

Applying for a Firearm Certificate

Demonstrate a Requirement
Individuals must show that they have reasonable cause to own and use a rifle. Being a member of a registered rifle club is a suitable reason, but this must be proved with a letter of confirmation signed by a registered club secretary. Membership is required at most clubs for a set period (usually a few months) before they will provide a letter.

Provide References
The Firearms Acts require an applicant for the grant or renewal of a Firearm Certificate to supply the names and addresses of two people who have agreed to act as referees. There are many conditions concerning who can and cannot be a referee; details can be

---

Prohibitions

It is an offence under section 21 of the Firearms Act of 1968, as amended, for anyone convicted of a criminal offence to handle, possess or shoot a firearm and ammunition (this includes air guns). If the sentence was for more than three years the prohibition is for life; if less than three years the prohibition is for five years. (Note that it is the sentence, not the time served, that is the determining factor.)

---

found on the FAC application form. The referees will be asked to complete a questionnaire about the applicant and return it directly to the police.

Storing a Rifle

If applying for an FAC with the general purpose of purchasing and owning a rifle, then assurances need to be made that the rifle will be stored securely. A proper gun cabinet/safe is required and must be fixed with coach bolts to a solid wall inside the permanent address of the applicant. The safe must not be visible or easily accessible to intruders; a separate safe is required for ammunition and bolts.

The police force granting the FAC will expect a steel cabinet of at least 16swg, bolted to the floor or wall and secured with five-lever lock(s). Connection to an alarm would be a bonus and in some locations may be a requirement. If the premises have shared access, for example if it is in a block of flats, the requirements may be more stringent and an FAC may not be granted.

It is important to be aware that if stored at a home address only the person listed on the FAC may handle or have access to the rifles. Parents, partners and offspring cannot handle the rifles, even in the home, unless they have their own FAC that lists the rifles as being in their possession.

PROGRESSING TO INTERMEDIATE LEVEL

There are no official definitions that determine who is a beginner, an intermediate level or an expert shooter. The boundary between the levels is often a matter of perspective. Although this book has covered beginner level theory for prone rifle shooting, it may also be useful to

---

Important note

The information given in this section is for guidance only. Anyone looking to apply for a Firearm Certificate must check the full and current laws with their local police firearms unit.

---

some who define themselves as being above beginner.

The boundaries between 'levels' can be defined by the number of years' experience a person has, by the level of their ability (club up to international) or by a combination of these factors. This makes it difficult to determine when a shooter progresses from the beginner to intermediate level. Someone who has only recently started shooting is certainly a beginner, even if they have a good level of ability. Similarly someone who has shot for thirty years may have a lot of experience but is not necessarily an expert owing to their limited level of knowledge of the sport, and so could be described as an intermediate level shooter.

Whatever the level a shooter is at, they should be able to find support and guidance for their shooting development from the club where they shoot and from the local, county and regional small-bore rifle associations.

For the reader who has reached the end of this book the next steps are to keep practising the core skills of breathing, aiming, trigger control and follow through. Shooting in competitions and attending events will also help build experience and knowledge of both indoor and outdoor shooting, while refining the prone position until smaller and more consistent groups are achieved.

FURTHER READING

Publications

Bühlmann, G., H. Reinkemeier, M. Eckhardt, B. Murray and A. Bindra, *Ways of the Rifle*, 2009 (MEC High Tech Shooting Equipment GmbH, 2008).

Meili, L., *Rifle: Steps to Success* (Human Kinetics, Inc, 2009).

Reinkemeier, H., *On the Training of Shooters*, trans. B. Murray and S. Greer, 2 vols (National Small-bore Rifle Association, 1992–3).

Yur'yev, A. A., *Competitive Shooting*, trans. G. L. Anderson (National Rifle Association of America, 1985).

Websites

http://www.issf-sports.org/theissf/history.ashx. History of the International Shooting Sport Federation (accessed 11 May 2010).

http://www.nsra.co.uk. Website of the National Small-bore Rifle Association.

http://www.carl-walther.de/index.php?company=walther&lang=EN&content=unternehmen&sub=historie. History of Carl Walther GmbH (accessed 11 May 2010).

http://jga.anschuetz-sport.com. Website of J. G. Anschütz GmbH & Co. KG.

USEFUL ADDRESSES

United Kingdom Governing Body
National Small-bore Rifle Association
Lord Roberts Centre
Bisley Camp
Brookwood
Woking
Surrey
GU24 0NP

Tel: 01483 485505
Fax: 01483 476392
www.nsra.co.uk

England
English Small-bore Shooting Union (ESSU)
www.essu.org.uk

Scotland
Scottish Smallbore Rifle Association (SSRA)
www.ssra.co.uk

Wales
Welsh Target Shooting Federation (WTSF)
www.wtsf.org.uk

Ireland
National Target Shooting Association of Ireland
89 Hillside
Greystones
Co. Wicklow
Ireland

Email: Secretary@targetshootingireland.org
www.targetshootingireland.org

USA
National Rifle Association of America
11250 Waples Mill Road
Fairfax
VA 22030
United States of America

Tel: 1-800-672-3888
www.nrahq.org

Australia
Target Tifle Association Australia
Fax: 0246551073
trasec@bigpond.com
www.tra.org.au

Germany
Deutscher Schützenbund e.V.
Lahnstraße 120
65195 Wiesbaden
Germany

Tel: 0611 46807-0
Fax: 0611 46807-49
info@dsb.de
www.dsb.de

INDEX